ALED JONES'
FORTY FAVOURITE HYMNS

ALED JONES' FORTY FAVOURITE HYMNS

ALED JONES

preface
publishing

Published by Preface 2009

10 9 8 7 6 5 4 3 2 1

First published in Great Britain in 2009 by Preface Publishing
20 Vauxhall Bridge Road
London SW1V 2SA

An imprint of The Random House Group Limited

www.rbooks.co.uk
www.prefacepublishing.co.uk

Addreses for companies within The Random House Group Limited
can be found at www.randomhouse.co.uk

The Random House Group Limited Reg. No. 954009

A CIP catalogue record for this book is available from the British Library

ISBN 978 1 84809 106 1

The Random House Group Limited supports The Forest Stewardship Council (FSC),
the leading international forest certification organisation. All our titles that are
printed on Greenpeace approved FSC certified paper carry the FSC logo.
Our paper procurement policy can be found at www.rbooks.co.uk/environment

Mixed Sources
Product group from well-managed
forests and other controlled sources
www.fsc.org Cert no. TT-COC-2139
© 1996 Forest Stewardship Council

Printed and bound in Great Britain by Clays Ltd, St Ives PLC

To Emilia and Lucas with all my love.

CONTENTS

Introduction ix

INTRODUCTION

T HE WORD HYMN comes from the Greek *hymnos*, meaning a song of praise. When I was asked to come up with
a book detailing the stories behind my forty favourite hymns,
and my anecdotes of performing them I thought to myself –
'Praise be! As an ex-chorister this should be an enjoyable and
easy experience.' I was wrong! It's only now that I look at
the finished volume in front of me, with my favourite hymns
listed from one through to forty, that I realize I haven't
included the great hymn 'O Worship the King', or 'To Be a
Pilgrim', or 'Shall We Gather at the River', or 'Rock of Ages'.
I haven't even got 'For All the Saints' or 'Come Down Oh
Love Divine' on the list, even though Ralph Vaughan Williams
is probably one of my most loved composers. And how about
'Oh For a Thousand Tongues'? No, that hasn't made the top
forty either!

What I appreciate now, having completed this book of my
favourites is that it should really be a top 100 or even more.
What I hadn't taken into account was just how much I like
hymns and how important they have been and continue to be
in my life. There are so many great hymns that could have
made it onto the list, but what I have included here are hymns
that I've sung throughout my life, from schooldays through to
my time at Bangor Cathedral and then returning to hymns and
religion through *Songs of Praise* and as a recording artist. Not a
day has gone by since beginning this journey that I haven't
agonized over what to include. My sincere apologies if your
particular favourite isn't included.

I pride myself on being an emotional singer and am not embarrassed to say that I feel good when I'm singing from the heart. Most of these hymns have moved me emotionally during performance. Some I still don't feel I've totally done justice to yet, but will try again in the future, 'Battle Hymn of the Republic' being just one example.

I've sung the majority of these pieces of music since being a toddler. I remember having an ingrown eyelash operation at the age of two-and-a-half, then coming back to my grand-mother's house and the only thing I wanted to do was stand on her dining-room table singing hymns while she accom-panied me on the piano. Such is the power of this spiritual music, it's remained with me throughout my life.

Most of the hymns that have made it into my top forty have amazing, almost other-worldly stories attached to them. Quite a few of them, especially as far as the melodies are concerned, have tales about being written in great haste – as if the composer, just like Mozart, was taking instant dictation from God! – a spontaneous outpouring as it were. Life-changing melodies have been written in a matter of minutes – often scribbled down on anything that was close to hand – even on parchment. It's hard to believe that they've now become standards used throughout the world as a bridge to Heaven.

I've been fascinated by the histories of some of our greatest hymns and have found it so interesting that in many instances the words and music have not come from the same source and that quite often the hymns we love to sing today have words and music written centuries apart. Knowing the stories behind them makes you value the quality and the power of the hymn more profoundly. Each hymn contains a wealth of valuable and challenging information that can only enrich our spiritual lives.

Two modern hymns have made it into the book because I think they also have that perfect marriage of words and music and I genuinely believe that they will be around for future generations to enjoy. I know that some traditionalists believe that some of the contemporary worship songs that we sing are lacking in invention and heart; but I think the two I've chosen, 'In Christ Alone' and 'Shine Jesus Shine' do sit very comfortably with the old greats.

There's nothing better than singing hymns in the company of like-minded people; being part of a congregation in a church, chapel or cathedral environment. But I've sung hymns in all manner of places – in studios, on cruise liners, concert halls in Europe, America, Japan and Australia, and even on the terraces, including 'Abide With Me' at Wembley Stadium. But some of my greatest hymn memories come from singing in the home of Welsh Rugby Union, in Cardiff. I hope people will enjoy reading what it's like to sing hymns like 'Guide Me O Thou Great Redeemer' or 'Calon Lan' in front of 65,000 people while standing on the pitch of the Millenium Stadium, when you can actually feel people's breath hit you with the passion of their performance. Infinitely more passion than in the crowd rendition of the Tom Jones hit 'Delilah', which is often also performed! I remember being totally overwhelmed by the experience. But what must it be like if you're actually playing in the match? I've been lucky enough to talk to rugby greats like Gareth Edwards and they tell me exactly what it's like, that it can spur you on to win a match. That's how powerful hymns are.

Even if you're not a Christian these hymns will have had an

impact on your life at some time or another. That's what makes *Songs of Praise* the greatest karaoke programme in the world. We all like to sing along to these catchy hits. We've all grown up with them – they're part of our being, they're ingrained in our souls. Even if we're not religious, chances are we've sung hymns at christenings, weddings or funerals.

I feel inspired when I sing hymns and many of the worship songs in this book have also inspired generations of song-writers to try to emulate those before them. It's been said that if you took a cross section of the world's most successful songwriters from all genres and asked them what makes the perfect song, nobody would really know the definitive answer. Maybe it really boils down to having a very catchy melody, a hook, a piece of music that stimulates and that everyone can sing. Add to that, timeless words that have global meaning and that's it – a masterpiece. The masterpieces in this book have stood the test of time through the millennia and they still have the ability to move people to achieve greatness in their lives. I see them very much as God's little gifts.

HOW GREAT THOU ART

Words: Carl Gustav Boberg (1859–1940)
Translation: Stuart K. Hine (1899–1989)
Music: Swedish folk tune

O Lord my God! When I in awesome wonder
Consider all the works Thy hands have made,
I see the stars, I hear the mighty thunder,
Thy power throughout the universe displayed.

Then sings my soul, my Saviour God, to Thee;
How great Thou art, how great Thou art!
Then sings my soul, my Saviour God, to Thee:
How great Thou art, how great Thou art!

When through the woods and forest glades I wander
And hear the birds sing sweetly in the trees;
When I look down from lofty mountain grandeur
And hear the brook and feel the gentle breeze:

Chorus

And when I think that God, His Son not sparing,
Sent Him to die, I scarce can take it in;
That on the cross, my burden gladly bearing,
He bled and died to take away my sin:

Chorus

When Christ shall come with shouts of acclamation
And take me home, what joy shall fill my heart!
Then I shall bow in humble adoration,
And there proclaim, my God, how great Thou art!

Chorus

LIKE BEETHOVEN's Pastoral Symphony, this popular hymn (voted the nation's favourite in the *Songs of Praise* poll) springs from the experience of a summer storm and the calm that follows. On a summer afternoon in 1885 a young Swede Carl Gustav Boberg, was walking home with friends from church near Kronoback in south-east Sweden. 'It was that time of year when everything seemed to be in its richest colouring,' he said, 'the birds were singing in trees and every-where . . . a thunderstorm appeared on the horizon and soon thunder and lightning. We had to hurry to shelter. But the storm was soon over and the clear sky appeared.'

'When I came home I opened my window toward the sea. There evidently had been a funeral and the bells were playing the tune of "When eternity's clock calling my saved soul to its Sabbath rest." That evening I wrote the song, "O Store Gud",' which means "O Good God". Boberg's verses were set to a Swedish folk tune and its first public performance was in a Varmland church in 1888.

Boberg was born in Monsteras, near Kalmar, the son of a carpenter. He worked for the church as a lay minister and wrote many hymns and gospel songs. He was editor of a Christian newspaper, *Sanningsvittnet* (Witness of the Truth);

the words and music of 'O Store Gud' were first published there in 1891. Boberg was also a politician and was for nearly twenty years, between 1912 and 1931, a Swedish parliamentarian.

'How Great Thou Art' has migrated into so many languages through its history that it can safely be described as a multinational hymn. An early, 1907, version in German was translated into Russian in 1912 by Ivan S. Prochanov, the 'Martin Luther of Russia'. It has also been translated into Welsh, Chinese, Japanese, Polish, Romanian, Spanish, Vietnamese, even Esperanto – twice. A Maori version, 'Whakaaria mai', was sung for Queen Elizabeth during her visit to New Zealand in 1981, and went on to spend six months in the New Zealand charts.

Today's version of 'How Great Thou Art' in English owes its origins to both a Salvation Army missionary and a country music singer. Stuart K. Hine was an Englishman dedicated to God in the Salvation Army, who with his wife Edith served as an evangelist missionary in Eastern Europe. While they were in Ukraine they discovered Ivan Prochanov's Russian version of the hymn and translated it.

Hine published his final four-verse version of the hymn in his gospel magazine *Grace and Peace*; thus it travelled the world from North America to Africa in the baggage of refugees and missionaries – and its travels continued until it came into the hands of Vernon 'Tim' Spencer (1908–1974).

Tim Spencer was born in Missouri and raised in Oklahoma. He was first and foremost a musician, who came to perform and write songs for the famous country group, Sons of the Pioneers (alongside Leonard Slye, who became the cowboy movie star Roy Rogers). They sang mainly cowboy songs, recording and performing on radio and in the movies to an America recovering from the Great Depression. They also established record label Manna Music in Burbank and in 1955, Spencer bought 'How Great Thou Art' from Stuart K. Hine for Manna Music, which made the song available to all, free of charge.

It is this version of the hymn that was 'sung one hundred times' during the 1957 Billy Graham Crusade in Madison Square Garden, 'because the people wouldn't let them stop.' And it became the signature song of the 1950s Billy Graham Crusades.

Billy Graham himself noted: 'The reason I like "How Great Thou Art" is because it . . . turns Christians' eyes toward God, rather than upon themselves.'

Elvis liked it too. He sang and recorded 'How Great Thou Art' frequently, notably as the title song of the musical album recorded at RCA Studios in Nashville in May 1966, which won a Grammy Award in 1967 in the Best Sacred Performance category and reached number 18 in the Billboard album charts.

And the former MP Anne Widdecombe likes it. She chose my performance of it on BBC Radio 4's 'Desert Island Discs' and I surprised her in the House of Commons with a live performance to celebrate her 60th birthday. A very surreal but enjoyable experience!

It's the nation's favourite hymn for a reason; it has immense power and heartfelt tenderness in equal measure. It's also loved by young and old because its been constructed in such a simple, effective way. The opening verse hits you straight away – four lines that celebrate God's mighty ability, followed by an immense statement of fellowship and praise.

O Lord My God! When I in awesome wonder
Consider all the works Thy hands have made,
I see the stars, I hear the mighty thunder,
Thy power throughout the universe displayed

Then sings my soul, my Saviour God, to thee:
How great Thou art, how great Thou art!

I usually leave out the verse about 'the woods and forest glades' when I perform this hymn. Instead, I go directly to the verse that sums up the gospel message superbly – I usually sing this in a much more understated and tender way – very reverential in approach. This is my private moment with my God on stage as I stare out into the darkness.

And when I think that God, his Son not sparing,
Sent Him to die, I scarce can take it in;
That on the cross, my burden gladly bearing,
He bled and died to take away my sin.

Then it's a huge dynamic change for the final verse – and even a key change if you're brave enough! and I love the line: 'And take me home, what joy shall fill my heart!' It's a warm, content feeling I love to share with the audience.

The final chorus is as majestic and grand as any hymn that's been written before or after. I end it on a belted high note, which is at the top of my vocal register. It is usually the loudest and most powerful note I've sung during the concert. The effort I put in is usually my way of saying thanks to God for allowing me to perform to my best in front of an appreciative audience.

'How Great Thou Art' means the world to me – I've sung it more times than any other hymn or song. Since coming out of retirement as a boy soprano and venturing back onto the platform as a Baritone, I've ended every single concert – that's well over five hundred – with this masterpiece. It invariably gets a standing ovation – that's down to the quality of the hymn, not me!

2

DEAR LORD AND FATHER OF MANKIND

Words: John Greenleaf Whittier (1807–92)
Music: Hubert Parry (1848–1918): *Repton*

Dear Lord and Father of mankind,
Forgive our foolish ways;
Reclothe us in our rightful mind;
In purer lives thy service find,
In deeper reverence, praise.

In simple trust like theirs who heard
Beside the Syrian sea
The gracious calling of the Lord
Let us, like them, without a word
Rise up and follow thee.

O Sabbath rest by Galilee!
O calm of hills above,
Where Jesus knelt to share with thee
The silence of eternity,
Interpreted by love!

With that deep hush subduing all
Our words and works that drown
The tender whisper of thy call,
As noiseless let thy blessing fall
As fell thy manna down.

Drop thy still dews of quietness,
Till all our strivings cease;
Take from our souls the strain and stress,
And let our ordered lives confess
The beauty of thy peace.

Breathe through the heats of our desire
Thy coolness and thy balm;
Let sense be dumb, let flesh retire,
Speak through the earthquake, wind, and fire,
O still small voice of calm!

I T'S HARD TO IMAGINE how one of our most popular hymns – consistently among the top three in the BBC *Songs of Praise* polls – came to be extracted from a poem all about a hallucinogenic drug! Do stay with me, I haven't lost the plot!

Soma was an intoxicating drink made from an Indian plant and used in early religious rituals to create a state of frenzy – it was a drug of religious choice in Vedic cultures, mentioned in the Rigveda, the ancient Indian sacred collection of Vedic Sanskrit hymns. John Greenleaf Whittier was not a follower of these practices, on the contrary, he was an American Quaker, a poet who wrote 'The Brewing of Soma' in 1872 to express his dislike of over-enthusiastic Christianity, with its use of 'music, incense, vigils drear, And trance, to bring the skies more near'. The Soma-induced state, he thought, could be compared with these rather unrestrained performances. The words of the poem that precede the verses of 'Dear Lord and Father of Mankind' express this:

> In sensual transports wild as vain
> We brew in many a Christian fane
> The heathen Soma still!

Written by a Quaker used to worshipping God in the 'calm', 'silence' and 'deep hush' of the meeting house, 'The Brewing of Soma' is a plea to 'Forgive our foolish ways' and 'Reclothe us in our rightful mind'. He was calling Christians back to simple pure worship.

Whittier grew up in the Quaker community around Haverhill in Massachusetts. He was a descendent of the Pilgrim Fathers and the son of farmers. With his roots firmly in Quakerism, he made his living as a journalist, wrote good poetry, and was a passionate abolitionist through his adult life.

Whittier has been credited as a fine hymn-writer, though he never wrote a hymn. He confessed, 'I am really not a hymn writer, for the good reason that I know nothing of music'. Many hymns have been drawn from his poetry; including the abolitionist 'O brother Man, fold to thy heart thy brother', and 'Dear Lord and Father of Mankind'.

From its strange beginnings, Whittier's poem travelled through various hands before it became the fully formed 'Dear Lord and Father of Mankind'. The great hymnologist William Garrett Horder (1841–1922) saw the potential of Whittier's verses and adapted them into the hymn 'Dear Lord and Father of Mankind', including it in his 1884 *Congregational Hymns*.

C. Hubert H. Parry, a very fine choral composer probably best known for his setting of William Blake's poem *Jerusalem*, in 1888 wrote an oratorio, *Judith*, which contained the aria, 'Long since in Egypt's pleasant land'. Parry's pupil George Gilbert Stocks, then director of music at Repton School, took the melody of this aria and set it to Horder's words, to be sung by Repton schoolboys in the school chapel.

The hymn can be sung to *Rest* by Frederick C. Maker (1844–1927): In the US, the hymn is generally sung to *Woodland* by Nathaniel Gould (1781–1864). But *Repton* is my melody of choice.

'Dear Lord and Father of Mankind' is the hymn sung by the exhausted soldier-choir in the bandstand on the beach at Dunkirk in *Atonement*, the 2007 film based on Ian McEwan's novel. The film won an Academy Award for best score. But to be fair it has been used to great effect on stage and screen many times.

During my time as a chorister at Bangor Cathedral it grew to be one of my favourites. Even though the Parry tune and Whittier words weren't really meant to go together, George Stocks at Repton School inadvertently created a masterpiece that stirs the soul to give a passionate performance. There is so much light and shade to be found in the words and melody, soaring passages that seem to deliver you closer to heaven as well as quiet intense phrases that make the hairs on the back of your neck stand up.

It's a very popular hymn to be sung at weddings – I was lucky enough to perform it at the fabulous wedding of Paula Yates to Bob Geldof, in their own private church no less! Bob particularly liked the line 'forgive our foolish ways'. It was an incredible experience looking up during my solo and seeing some of the world's most recognizable rock and pop stars either singing along heartily or in floods of tears. There were some very talented songwriters in the congregation but not one of them could have written such an emotionally stirring popular song.

As a child singer, this was one of the last hymns I ever put down to tape – a bittersweet memory. It had appeared on some of my albums before but on 29 December 1986 my producers in St Augustine's church in Penarth decided that as a treat I could also include it on what was to become my last unfinished CD.

As a boy in my prime singing this near perfect hymn was like playing football in the school playground – effortless. I prided myself on being able to almost sing an entire verse in one breath. That morning in Penarth, with my mother and two BBC producers outside the church in a recording van, the hymn 'Dear Lord and Father of Mankind' proved to be my undoing. Due to the fact that the tune sat in my middle vocal register I found it nearly impossible to sing even one phrase without gulping for air. I wasn't aware at the time but my voice had obviously started to break! I have very vivid memories of asking all assembled in the van via intercom if my voice sounded alright. The reply was always an encouraging, 'No problems at all,' or, 'Yeah, sounds fine'. The truth was that producers, engineer and mum were all in tears. They were all too aware what was happening. We went for an early lunch and never went back to finish the album. The hymn 'Dear Lord and Father of Mankind' was the last piece of music I sang as a boy soprano.

This rather poignant occasion is not where my professional association with this gloriously expressive hymn ends. Since returning to professional singing and recording I have performed it many times. The highlight was on my second adult album, *Higher*. I'd uncovered a previously unheard child-recording of mine of the hymn and decided to duet with myself! I went into the studio and recorded the adult 'part' and when my producer played the child and adult voices together, you could hear that the phrasing and emotional content in both performances was identical. 'Dear Lord and Father of Mankind' was the proof I needed that boy had officially turned into man!

3

MAKE ME A CHANNEL
OF YOUR PEACE

Words and music: Sebastian Temple (1928–1997)

Make me a channel of your peace.
Where there is hatred, let me bring your love.
Where there is injury, your pardon, Lord.
And where there's doubt, true faith in you.

Make me a channel of your peace.
Where there's despair in life, let me bring hope.
Where there is darkness, only light.
And where there's sadness, ever joy.

Oh, Master grant that I may never seek
So much to be consoled as to console,
To be understood as to understand,
To be loved, as to love with all my soul.

Make me a channel of your peace.
It is in pardoning that we are pardoned,
In giving of ourselves that we receive
And in dying that we're born to eternal life.

S O MANY OF THE marvellous hymns celebrated in this book
have been written and composed by seekers, who've had
to journey in body and soul like Bunyan's Pilgrim, to find God

and religious truth: John Newton sailed the seas, the life of John Henry Newman seems to me itself a sort of spiritual journey.

The words of this simple hymn are of peace and reconciliation, but it is also rooted in an unusual journey. Sebastian Temple adapted the words from 'The Prayer of St Francis', and composed the music for the hymn. His travels took him from Pretoria in South Africa, through Europe and England, and finally to California. He grew up a Catholic among Calvinists and left home in his teens – to Italy and thence to London, where his years in Pretoria stood him in good stead with the BBC, which hired him for his knowledge of South African affairs. He travelled onward to the United States and in the late fifties took up Scientology, but that did not help him to find a purpose for his life; he returned to the Catholic faith and settled into a secular order of Franciscans on the West Coast, where he found his vocation, writing and composing music for worship. Among the many hymns and songs Sebastian Temple had recorded by his death in 1997, 'Make Me a Channel of Your Peace' is considered a modern classic.

It is based closely on the words of The Peace Prayer of St Francis, whose origins are mysterious because it was discovered written on the back of a holy card of St Francis during the First World War. Although not the work of St Francis, I think it shines with his simplicity.

> Lord, make me an instrument of your peace.
> Where there is hatred let me sow love;
> Where there is injury, pardon;
> Where there is doubt, faith;
> Where there is despair, hope;
> Where there is darkness, light.

O Divine Master grant that I may not so much
  seek to be consoled
As to console;
To be understood, as to understand;
To be loved, as to love.
For it is in giving that we receive,
It is in pardoning that we are pardoned,
And it is in dying that we are born to eternal life.

The prayer was first published during 1912 in *La Clochette* (The Little Bell), a diminutive French devotional bulletin, as a prayer for peace during war. It has been quoted in many contexts. When, for instance, Pope John Paul II arrived to address the United Nations in 1995, President Clinton repeated it in his welcoming speech. In the first *Rambo* movie, a priest blesses Sylvester Stallone in the words of the Prayer, and it's recited in *Band of Brothers* by the medic Eugene Roe. But its value always returns to the simplicity of everyday prayer: Mother Theresa made it part of the daily morning prayers of her Missionaries of Charity in Calcutta, and for Archbishop Desmond Tutu, it has, he says, been an 'integral part' of his devotions.

I think it could be said that St Francis of Assisi and his follower Sebastian Temple worked together on this hymn. Temple was struggling to find the music to fit the words. In a letter used by Ian Bradley, author of the *Daily Telegraph Book of Hymns*, he describes what happened:

. . . I tried for a whole morning but nothing came. Finally, I was disgusted, looked at the little statue of St Francis on my shelf and said angrily, 'Well, if you want to write it, YOU do it. I can't.' I got up, went to the

kitchen, made a cup of tea and drank it. When I
returned to the guitar, I picked it up, had the tape
running, and the song fell out of my mouth.

This is typical of St Francis, who was well known for his
generosity towards man and beast. The Fioretti, those legends
about Francis that followed his death in 1226, have it that he
talked to the birds. He also tamed the ferocious wolf that
terrorised the city of Gubbio, telling him: 'Brother wolf I
would like to make peace between you and the people.' And
did so. 'While you are proclaiming peace with your lips,' he
taught, 'be careful to have it even more fully in your heart.'
This hymn is inspired by St Francis' self-imposed task to quell
discord and it is his request to God that He make us a channel
of His peace.

I know that 'Make Me a Channel of Your Peace' is well
liked by the Royal British Legion, and is often sung at the
Legion's annual Service of Remembrance held in the Royal
Albert Hall. In 2008, the hymn was sung at the funeral in his
home village of a British soldier killed in Afghanistan.

Unbelievably, this isn't a hymn I recorded as a child; even
though there were sixteen albums full of hymns, for some
reason this one escaped me. It's become one of my favourite
pieces of music; it's very ballad-like in its construction, so not
as 'square' as some of the hymns can be. I recorded it on my
debut album as a man with the great Irish producer Christie
Hennessy, who's a fantastic singer-songwriter, unfortunately
no longer with us, producing the album.

It was very tricky to record, getting the sentiment right.
The words are very, very powerful and the melody also
incredibly beautiful. It was one of those sessions where it was

getting on for midnight, we'd recorded a couple of other pieces and Christie suggested that we turn all the lights off in the studio and it would just be myself and the pianist ad-libbing and performing together. There was a magic in that room at that precise moment as in the darkness the pianist started playing. I was instantly inspired. We did it all in one take. It was probably the most moving recording session I've ever had in my life. I think it's the one piece of music that I've captured to my one hundred per cent potential and since then I sing it all the time. It has a real journey – the fact that there are positive high moments and also very exposed moments. I've recorded it on several of my albums: with piano accompaniment, orchestra; I've even sung it unaccompanied.

I'm not one for breaking down on stage when I'm performing. I pride myself on being an emotional singer but I'm never close to tears on stage. I like being in total control on the platform.

That control went out of the window one night on tour in the Bridewater Hall in Manchester. I did cry during 'Make Me a Channel of Your Peace'. My uncle had died two days' earlier and my thoughts turned to him towards the end of the hymn. I'm convinced it's to do with the words: 'Where there is despair, hope / Where there is darkness, light' and also 'in giving that we receive', and the final line hit me, 'And it is in dying that we gain eternal life'. I said farewell to my beloved uncle at that moment, knowing that we would meet again. It was a mixture of feelings – sorrow and relief. There was something very poignant about it, lots of people commented at an autograph signing session afterwards. They obviously thought that I was acting, but it was the real thing.

I've heard this hymn sung in strict time, and I have to be honest and say that I'm not a fan of it performed in that way. I think that this hymn gives you the opportunity to put your heart into it, your own stamp on it. You can start it so quietly, so intimately. It's a straightforward request: 'Make me a channel of your peace / Where there is hatred let me bring your love', then build it up in the second verse, build it up in the third verse and even mess around with the time. I think that this is a hymn that you can be totally free with and only then does the true message comes across.

4

LOVE DIVINE

Words: Charles Wesley (1707–88)
Music: John Stainer (1840–1901): *Love Divine*
Music: Charles Villiers Stanford (1852–1924): *Airedale*
Music: William Penfro Rowlands (1860–1937): *Blaenwern*
Music: Rowland Huw Prichard (1811–57): *Hyfrydol*

Love divine, all loves excelling,
Joy of heaven, to earth come down,
Fix in us thy humble dwelling,
All thy faithful mercies crown.
Jesu, thou art all compassion,
Pure unbounded love thou art;
Visit us with thy salvation,
Enter every trembling heart.

(Breath, O breathe thy loving Spirit
Into every troubled breast,
Let us all in thee inherit,
Let us find that second rest;
Take away our power of sinning,
Alpha and Omega be,
End of faith, as its beginning,
Set our hearts at liberty.)

Come, almighty to deliver,
Let us all thy life receive;
Suddenly return, and never,
Never more thy temples leave.
Thee we would be always blessing,
Serve thee as thy hosts above,
Pray, and praise thee, without ceasing,
Glory in thy perfect love.

Finish then thy new creation,
Pure and spotless let us be;
Let us see thy great salvation,
Perfectly restored to thee:
Changed from glory into glory,
Till in heaven we take our place,
Till we cast our crowns before thee,
Lost in wonder, love, and praise!

'LOVE DIVINE' is one of Charles Wesley's finest and is definitely one of the nation's most popular hymns – perhaps because it dwells upon the idea of God as Love, a concept unusual in hymns of earlier times. It is also one of the top five hymns in the *Songs of Praise* countdown and it's right that it should be up there with 'Guide Me O Thou Great Redeemer', 'The Day Thou Gavest' and 'Dear Lord and Father of Mankind'.

Charles Wesley wrote around 6,000 hymns – I know what you're thinking, he didn't get out much! – but he did, he was a travelling preacher. Legend has it that he scribbled down hymn ideas on little cards that he carried with him as he rode.

Once a horse threw him off and this is what he wrote in his diary, 'My companion thought I had broken my neck, but my leg was only bruised, my hand sprained and my head stunned, which spoiled my making hymns the next day.' He was definitely someone who took his hymns seriously!

One of the many stories about Charles Wesley reveals a small part of the creative process that went into the writing of 'Love Divine'. It's said that he was inspired to write the hymn after hearing a popular song, 'The Song of Venus', written in 1691 by John Dryden for his play 'King Arthur' and set to music by Henry Purcell. These lyrics of a classical kind:

> Fairest Isle, all isles excelling,
> Seat of pleasures, and of loves;
> Venus here will choose her dwelling,
> And forsake her Cyprian groves.

Wesley turned into a Christian welcoming of the divine in our lives:

> Love divine, all loves excelling,
> Joy of heaven, to earth come down,
> Fix in us thy humble dwelling,
> All thy faithful mercies crown.

Charles Wesley's brother John made several changes to the hymn as Charles wrote it. The original composition consisted of four verses. A second verse was taken out by John, maybe because he disagreed with his brother's belief expressed in the hymn that we can be completely cleansed of sin in this life. He made several other alterations, some of which have been kept in the final version, and some not. For example, he wanted to change the second line of the fourth verse from 'Pure and sinless let us be' to 'Pure and spotless let us be'.

Despite the cutting of the original, the final version of this hymn is deservedly loved by all of us who sing it. It has a satisfying structure with its three verses expressing an exhortation for the Lord to come down to earth and 'enter every trembling heart'; the receiving of grace and giving of praise; and finally the glory of entering the kingdom of heaven.

There are so many different melodies to 'Love Divine', written by men from so many different backgrounds. These settings for the hymn include *Airedale* by Charles Villiers Stanford, an Irishman, composer of great virtuosity and teacher, whose pupils included the starry group of Gustav Holst, Ralph Vaughan Williams and John Ireland, and *Blaenwern,* written in 1905 by the humble schoolteacher William P. Rowlands. There's another Welsh tune, *Hyfrydol,* composed by Rowland Huw Prichard, who worked in the Welsh mills and was a choir director with a beautiful singing voice of his own. And there's John Stainer's version, *Love Divine.* Stainer was a well-respected organist and composer; he wrote the music for many hymns and was knighted by Queen Victoria. There are also more modern versions: by Howard Goodall, which I've sung, and William Lloyd Webber, who is Andrew and Julian's father, has written music for 'Love Divine' as well. I met up with composer Sir Philip Ledger recently. He was a guest on my BBC Radio 3 choral programme. He was born in Bexhill and educated at King's College, Cambridge. When appointed Master of Music at Chelmsford Cathedral, he became the youngest cathedral organist in the United Kingdom. As Director of Music at the

University of East Anglia, he worked closely with Benjamin Britten as an Artistic Director of the Aldeburgh Festival before returning to King's College, Cambridge as Director of Music. There he conducted the Festival of Nine Lessons and Carols which is broadcast each year on Christmas Eve, made an extensive range of recordings with the famous choir and directed recitals and tours throughout the world. He then became Principal of the Royal Scottish Academy of Music and Drama. I was aware that he had also set Wesley's words to music, so I asked him why. He said:

> 'The words of certain hymns seem to speak directly and in a very special way to our inner selves. "Love Divine" is one such and is frequently sung at weddings. For me, its very first line, *Love divine, all loves excelling* has an immediate appeal as does the last, *Lost in wonder, love, and praise*. Charles Wesley who wrote the hymn was almost certainly influenced by John Dryden whose famous words, *Fairest isle, all isles excelling* were set by Henry Purcell. The tune by John Stainer to "Love Divine" is known and loved by many but there are a number of others which admirably complement the noble and evocative words of this wonderful hymn.'

The two versions I've sung the most are the Stainer version and *Hyfrydol*, but my favourite would have to be *Blaenwern* because this tune really lends itself to the words and gives you a vocal and musical journey to go on. I've sung it in Bangor Cathedral and on *Songs of Praise* many times and have recorded this version on album. I haven't sung it in concert yet, but it's only a matter of time. It starts slowly and builds up through the verses but the highlight musically for me comes in the last

four lines of the last verse: 'Changed from glory into glory /
Till in heaven we take our place, / Till we cast our crowns
before thee / Lost in wonder, love and praise!'

I've had many a battle with musical directors and fellow
musicians over which tune is best for 'Love Divine' – it's
testament to the wonderful words that there are so many
great tunes. It's always a toss-up between *Blaenwern* and
Hyfrydol, both of course Welsh tunes!

5

GUIDE ME
O THOU GREAT REDEEMER

Words: William Williams (1717–91)
Translation: Peter Williams (1727–96)
Music: John Hughes (1873–1932): *Cwm Rhondda*

Guide me, O thou great Redeemer,
Pilgrim through this barren land;
I am weak, but thou art mighty,
Hold me with thy powerful hand:
Bread of heaven,
Feed me till I want no more.

Open thou the crystal fountain,
Whence the healing stream doth flow;
Let the fire and cloudy pillar
Lead me all my journey through:
Strong deliverer,
Be thou still my strength and shield.

When I tread the verge of Jordan,
Bid my anxious fears subside;
Death of death, and hell's destruction,
Land me safe on Canaan's side:
Songs of praises
I will ever give to thee.

FOR JOHN BETJEMAN, Welsh hymns have a special quality, 'a note of profound sorrow married to a deep reverence'*; this hymn, written by 'Y per ganiedydd', the 'sweet singer' from Llandovery, has that quality.

Betjeman called William Williams the 'Charles Wesley of Wales'. He was a Methodist preacher, who went on the road and travelled thousands of miles on foot and horseback, carrying the Word of God around Wales.

Williams came from farming stock around Llandovery. Pantycelyn, his family's farmhouse, gave him the name he came to be known by: William Williams 'Pantycelyn'. He set out to be a doctor, but was stopped in his tracks when he heard the powerful preaching of the Calvinist Howell Harris and was from that day caught up in the movement to bring back evangelicism to Wales. Williams preached out of doors and was known to captivate his audiences and confound the local establishment, who labelled him a rabble-rouser and were unsettled by the opening words of the hymn – the original ones: 'Arglwydd, arwain trwy'r anialwch', 'Guide me, O thou great Jehovah' – fearing this was a sign of their impending overthrow. He wrote abundantly, poems and hymns on religious themes. He noted down this hymn in 1756. Within the hymn he is what he was in life, a pilgrim, sharing the epic journey of the Israelites who followed Moses through the barren lands to Canaan.

This bible story is a rich one, full of drama and symbolism. It's found in Exodus 13–17, where the children of Israel received manna, the 'bread of heaven', to keep them going: 'Then said the Lord unto Moses, Behold I will rain bread

*John Betjeman in *Sweet Songs of Zion*

from heaven for you'; and to drink, water from the 'Crystal fountain', as God tells Moses, 'Behold I will stand before thee upon the rock in Horeb; and thou shalt smite the rock, and there shall come water out of it, that the people may drink.' The Israelites' beacon is the 'fiery cloudy pillar': 'And the Lord went before them by day and night: he took not away the pillar of the cloud by day, nor the pillar of fire by night.'

Wales of course has provided the world with many magnificent hymn tunes, but few with words that have been translated from the Welsh language into English – 'Guide Me O Thou Great Redeemer' is one of the exceptions. Most of the hymn is to be attributed to Peter Williams of Carmarthen's translation, no relative of William, but his contemporary. It was published in 1771; a year later a version was included in a leaflet of hymns with the note, 'A favourite hymn sung by Lady Huntington's Young Collegians'.

'Guide Me O Thou Great Redeemer' was set to a number of tunes until in 1905 another Welshman, John Hughes, composed *Cwm Rhondda* ('Rhondda Valley') for a Baptist singing festival at Pontypridd. He was a precentor at his church there, and he worked on the Great Western Railway. The unlikely tale is told that he picked up a tarpaulin and wrote the music on it.

It has also, as my colleague at the BBC Andrew Barr has pointed out, been associated with lives of the Welsh miners in the Rhondda, who would sing *Cwm Rhondda* during their daily work at the coalfield. This was represented in film when Richard Llewellyn's 1939 novel about the coming of age of Huw Morgan in a South Wales mining community was made into a film – *How Green Was My Valley* (1941), directed by John Ford and filmed on a reconstruction of a mining town in

Malibu Canyon, USA. Alfred Newman arranged the hymn and won a 1941 Academic Award for Original Music Score, one of the five Awards won by the film.

Cwm Rhondda has made this hymn famous, sung by church-goers around the world. On 6 September 1997, it was sung in Westminster Abbey at the funeral of Diana, Princess of Wales – by the full congregation – and on 9 April 2002 at the funeral of Queen Elizabeth the Queen Mother. On a lighter note I chose this hymn for my wedding service.

Again in Westminster Abbey, in 2001, the London Welsh Male Voice Choir led the singing of this hymn during the memorial to celebrate the life of the Welsh singer and Goon Sir Harry Secombe, whose favourite it was. It was a privilege for me to be there on that occasion. It was so fitting that this great hymn should be chosen to honour a great man.

Appropriately, given the lifestyle of its author, 'Guide Me O Thou Great Redeemer' has a history of being performed out of doors. A legend has it that the Welsh soldiers in the Flanders trenches sung it so beautifully that the entrenched German troops sang it too. It is the hymn sung at rugby matches when the national Wales rugby team is in action and was sung at the opening of Wales's national Millennium Stadium in June 1999.

I have been fortunate enough to sing this hymn at the Millennium Stadium before a Wales rugby fixture – an incredible experience never to be matched. Due to inclement weather the roof of the stadium had been closed, so as you can imagine the sound of 60,000 plus Welsh voices in full throw was exhilarating. I have never felt so emotional during a performance. Over the years I have got to know quite a few of my Welsh rugby heroes – Cliff Morgan, Gareth Edwards and the late Ray Gravell to name but a few. They all say the same thing – hearing the uplifting strains of 'Bread of Heaven' coming from the stands definitely spurs the team on to greatness. Gareth commented that it was the equivalent of instantly adding an extra three points onto the Welsh score!

British football crowds like the hymn too, but sing it without reverence: 'You're not singing anymore' . . . 'feed the goat and he will score' and more. I remember as a teenager standing on the terraces in my beloved Highbury, home of Arsenal football club. It had only recently been announced that my voice had broken. Standing there in amongst 9,000 or so fellow supporters I was left speechless and very red faced as what felt like the whole stadium spontaneously started chanting – 'Aled Jones, Aled Jones, You're not singing any more'! Needless to say I was very embarrassed but looking back it was a very special moment in my life.

In 2008 BBC 1 put on a show 'to find the nation's favourite choir'. Over 1,000 choirs entered for *Last Choir Standing*, which as the name suggests was an exhausting, hard fought contest. Last standing was the Cardiff-based Only Men Aloud. Their chosen repertoire was mostly secular; they performed 'Don't Rain on My Parade' from *Funny Girl*, 'All by Myself' by Eric Carmen – and finally *Cwm Rhondda*. An inspired choice as God maybe came to be on their side.

6

BE STILL FOR THE PRESENCE OF THE LORD

Words and Music: David J Evans (1957–)

Be still,
For the presence of the Lord,
The Holy One, is here;
Come bow before Him now
With reverence and fear:
In Him no sin is found –
We stand on holy ground.
Be still,
For the presence of the Lord,
The Holy One, is here.

Be still,
For the glory of the Lord
Is shining all around;
He burns with holy fire,
With splendour He is crowned:
How awesome is the sight –
Our radiant King of light!
Be still,
For the glory of the Lord
Is shining all around.

Be still,

For the power of the Lord

Is moving in this place:

He comes to cleanse and heal,

To minister His grace –

No work too hard for Him.

In faith receive from Him

Be still,

For the power of the Lord,

Is moving in this place.

D AVID EVANS wrote 'Be Still For the Presence of the Lord' in 1985 – apparently in a single evening. This remarkable and very popular hymn, which is currently number three in the Christian Copyright Licensing UK chart, is absolutely in the now, where we are being asked to share its author's direct experience of God's presence.

David Evans' father was in the Army, so as a child he must have moved with his family on many occasions; his hymn encourages us to do the opposite and to come into a place of stillness. It is the ideal hymn to be used, as it often is, for retreat and reflection.

'Be Still' was introduced to me by Robert Prizeman, who is the music supervisor on *Songs of Praise*. He's also the producer of my first three records with Universal that I recorded when I came back to presenting *Songs of Praise*. I'd never heard this piece of music until he played it for me and I was instantly struck by its beauty. I've since performed it thousands of times on platforms here in Britain and as far afield as Australia. This is the piece of music I always choose in my concerts hopefully to take the audience to another dimension, to another place. I've performed it accompanied by organ, I've also performed it with string quartet and keyboard, even guitar.

There are three verses. What I love is that each verse takes you on a particular journey. The first verse I often perform in a quite simple way, but again it's not hymn-like in its construction, it's definitely not metered. This is a worship song that you can put your own stamp on and I hope I have done that. I love the ethereal quality of the first verse 'Come bow before Him now / With reverence and fear / In Him no sin is found / We stand on holy ground / Be still / For the presence of the Lord / The Holy one is here'. It's asking us to stop what we're doing for a couple of minutes each day and actually take in who we are and why we're on this earth, which is quite tricky to do especially in my life, which is constantly on the go with motorbikes, cars, trains and planes here there and everywhere. Actually this is one piece of music where you listen to the first chord before coming in with 'Be still for the presence of the Lord', and you feel the pressures of the day just dripping off you.

In the second verse we're talking about the glory of the Lord so it requires a little more voice, a little more intensity: 'He burns with holy fire / With splendour He is crowned', so the words are a lot more praise-like in their quality. 'Our radiant king of light' and the fact that the 'glory of the Lord is shining all around' are lines I love to sing. So in the first verse we're talking about the presence of the Lord, everywhere you look He is there and then you're being reminded that when you have stood still for a while, actually it's the glory of the Lord that you're experiencing. But you won't get to experience the glory without first being still. And then the third verse – wait for it: 'the power of the Lord is moving in this place', that's one of the most powerful lines for me. When I sing it either in a cathedral or in a concert hall I really try to convince those listening that God is actually present in what I'm doing and is present for them to share and acknowledge and be part of. 'Be still for the *power* of the Lord / is *moving* in this place'. Something spiritual is actually happening at that precise moment.

This is probably the piece of music I've recorded most on *Songs of Praise*; during my eight years as presenter I've probably made up to ten videos of 'Be Still'. Every time a producer rings up and asks if I fancy singing on the programme, I of course say yes and invariably their first choice will be 'Be Still For the Presence of the Lord'. I've sung it in Llanberis in Snowdonia in North Wales recently, which was a very moving experience, as I was almost on home turf. I suppose one of the most awe inspiring and emotional recordings of this piece on *Songs of Praise* was the one where I was walking in a church graveyard and all of a sudden I morph out of shot. In comes a sort of mini-me as a young child with a mop of blond hair, walking the exact same path that the adult Aled is walking. It's so touching seeing this young child walking around this beautiful church graveyard actually experiencing God's presence – as boy and man.

The choirboy sense of humour is never far away even now I'm supposedly an adult. When we were recording this piece of music we actually called it 'Beast Ill' and I always had a vision of a cow vomiting in a field somewhere in Wales. There, now you know!

So many of the songs in this book are most effective when there is repetition in the words. We've seen this with 'Praise Him, Praise Him' in 'Praise my Soul the King of Heaven' and here it's wonderful the way that David Evans achieves such a powerful message through the use of the two little words – 'Be still' – that are used at the beginning and end of each verse. I'm not sure how David would feel about this, but when I perform it in concert I then reinforce that message by ending on 'Be still' again. It's almost as if you're pleading with the people who are witnessing you perform it to actually partake of what you're going through and just get off the treadmill of life for a moment.

David, incidentally, views his own lyrics as unexceptional, which I totally disagree with. He also views the melody as uncomplicated. He might be right about the melody but I would add that the tune is also a complete joy to sing. Not to be melodramatic, but hand on heart I can say that 'Be Still For the Presence of the Lord' is one of a handful of pieces of music that when I perform it I feel that I have a personal connection with God.

This hymn means a great deal to me, it's always in my line-up for concerts due to the fact that it has an ethereal quality and that it can move audiences to a different place – heaven, I suppose. That's always the aim. We could all do with having this hymn in our lives.

7

AMAZING GRACE
(HOW SWEET THE SOUND)

Words: John Newton (1725–1807)
Music: American folk melody.

Amazing grace! how sweet the sound
That saved a wretch like me!
I once was lost, but now am found,
Was blind, but now I see.

T'was grace that taught my heart to fear,
And grace my fears relieved;
How precious did that grace appear
The hour I first believed.

Through many dangers, toils and snares
I have already come;
'Tis grace hath brought me safe thus far,
And grace will lead me home.

The Lord has promised good to me,
His word my hope secures;
He will my shield and portion be
As long as life endures.

Yes, when this flesh and heart shall fail,
And mortal life shall cease,
I shall possess within the veil
A life of joy and peace.

The earth shall soon dissolve like snow,
The sun forbear to shine,
But God, who called me here below,
Will be for ever mine.

When we've been there ten thousand years,
Bright shining like the sun,
We've no less days to sing God's praise,
Than when we've first begun.

JOHN NEWTON, author of this powerful hymn beloved of many denominations, had lived such a remarkable and riotous life before he sat down to write 'Amazing Grace' in the Olney Rectory that books have been written and films, even a musical, made about it.

John Newton was born in Wapping, London. He was a sailor born and bred; he went to sea with his father aged eleven and on to serve as midshipman aboard HMS *Harwich*. When he was eighteen he deserted and was caught, brought back in chains, flogged before his shipmates and demoted to common seaman. From this he went on to further tribulations, working on slave ships bound for Africa. He was eventually rescued from this life as 'a servant of slaves' and set sail for England on the *Greyhound* in 1748.

Newton's mother, who died when he was a child, had given him some religious convictions, but these he had lost during his life as 'an infidel and libertine'. However, on the voyage home a violent storm threatened the ship and all on it; Newton had what he called his 'great deliverance', calling to God 'to have mercy upon us. Thro' many dangers, toils and snares, I have already come', he noted, in words that 'Amazing Grace' echoes: 'tis grace has bro't me safe thus far, and grace will lead me home.'

In 1750 Newton married his long-time love Mary Catlett. Still he continued working the slave routes and only later in the century turned his talents to the abolition of the slave trade, advising William Wilberforce, and writing to support the campaign.

He was ordained into the Church of England in 1764 and made curate of Olney in Buckinghamshire, where his preaching attracted a large congregation, including the poet William Cowper. Newton and Cowper together produced a collection of hymns, published in 1779 as *Olney Hymns*. Two hundred and eighty of these are Newton's compositions, including this hymn and 'Glorious Things of Thee are Spoken'.

John Newton died in London on 21 December 1807 having served the Lord and his church faithfully for almost sixty years. When he was nearing the end of his life he said, 'My memory is nearly gone but I can remember two things; that I am a great sinner and that Christ is a great saviour'. The following words are found on his tombstone in the church-yard of his former parish at Olney: 'John Newton, clerk, once an infidel and libertine, a servant of slaves in Africa, was by the rich mercy of our Lord and Saviour, Jesus Christ, preserved, restored, pardoned and appointed to preach the faith he had long laboured to destroy'.

Newton's story has inspired many movies, stage

extravaganzas and novels. Albert Finney played John Newton as Willliam Wilberforce's (played by Ioan Gruffudd) mentor during his crusade for the abolition of slavery in Michael Apted's 2007 film *Amazing Grace*. Another film, also with the title *Amazing Grace*, released in 2006, directed by Jeta Amata, shows the African perspective on the subject and Caryl Phillips' novel *Crossing the River*, also with slavery as its theme, quotes from Newton's books. A musical, *Amazing Grace: The True Story*, is 'the epic saga of storms, slavery, romance and redemption based on the life of John Newton' (Christopher Smith).

'Amazing Grace' is very popular in America, where its musical roots are. Its tune is based in an American folk melody, published in 1831 in *Virginia Harmony*, harmonised for this hymn by Edwin O. Excell in his *Coronation Hymns* (1910). The hymn was sung by both sides in the American Civil War. It's also said that the Cherokee nation on the Trail of Tears from their homelands in the 1830s, sang the hymn when they were not able to give those who died on the journey a full burial. The last verse here is not by Newton, but it is a great one to sing. This verse was originally from a hymn called 'Jerusalem My Happy Home'. It was added to the original 'Amazing Grace' by Connecticut-born preacher and active abolitionist Harriet Beecher Stowe. It's quoted in her anti-slavery novel *Uncle Tom's Cabin*, published in 1852.

During the 1920s, African-American singing preachers took up the hymn, including Reverends J. M. Gates and J. C. Burnett. It has since been recorded many times and by many different artists: Aretha Franklin, Judy Collins, Elvis, Neil Diamond, Crystal Gayle, Kylie Minogue, Joan Baez, Hayley Westenra, Katherine Jenkins, the Pipes and Drums and

Military Band of the Royal Scots Dragoon Guards have all in their own styles made the hymn their own. There is the folk tradition of the hymn, made popular by Arthur Penn's 1969 film *Alice's Restaurant*, where the evangelical meeting's rendition is led by Lee Hays of The Weavers.

The bagpipes have in recent times been associated with 'Amazing Grace'. The Star Ship Enterprise's Scottie went where no man had gone before with the hymn, playing it on the bagpipes during Spock's funeral in *Star Trek II: The Wrath of Khan* (1982). Another bagpipe version was released by the Boston Irish punk band the Dropkick Murphys on their 1999 album 'The Gang's All Here'. It's not a version I listen to often on my MP3 player!

I was quite daunted when a producer suggested I record 'Amazing Grace'. It was to be included on my first 'adult' album. My first thought was: 'no way, as it's been done so many times before by so many great artistes' – how on earth would I make this hymn my own and put my stamp on it? I started practising but was struggling greatly. Then late one night mid flow it hit me – it was almost as if my prayer, like Newton's, had been answered – don't try to do any-thing clever or gimmicky, just sing the song. Trust in the message of the hymn. I honestly do believe that the way to perform 'Amazing Grace' is simply, honestly and with an open heart.

I went into the empty studio and recorded it with no band or accompaniment – it was done in one take!

It was around this time my beloved grandmother was very unwell in hospital. Even though she was ill, whenever my mother and father went to visit her she would enquire about how the recording session was going. I will never forget the call from my father informing me that my 'Nain' wasn't going to live much longer than a few days. She had remarked that she longed to hear something of the 'new' voice. I hurriedly did a rough mix of 'Amazing Grace' and couriered it off to North Wales. She had been one of my best friends in life and I am so proud that my voice, singing this extra-ordinary hymn, was the last music she heard – and I hope it helped her on her journey to heaven.

8

THE DAY THOU GAVEST, LORD, IS ENDED

Words: John Ellerton (1826–93)
Music: Clement Cotterill Scholefield (1839–1904)

The day thou gavest, Lord, is ended,
The darkness falls at thy behest;
To thee our morning hymns ascended,
They praise shall sanctify our rest.

We thank thee that thy Church unsleeping,
While earth rolls onward into light,
Through all the world her watch is keeping,
And rests not now by day or night.

As o'er each continent and island
The dawn leads on another day,
The voice of prayer is never silent,
Nor dies the strain of praise away.

The sun that bids us rest is waking
Our brethren 'neath the western sky,
And hour by hour fresh lips are making
Thy wondrous doings heard on high.

So be it, Lord; thy throne shall never,
Like earth's proud empires, pass away;
Thy kingdom stands, and grows for ever,
Till all thy creatures own thy sway.

B Y 1897, Queen Victoria had been Britain's sovereign for a remarkable sixty years, presiding over a country moving rapidly into the modern age, adapting to change and busy building her empire. On 22 June of that year, she celebrated her Diamond Jubilee at Westminster Abbey, and she chose one hymn for that service, which she also asked to be sung in thousands of churches across Britain. The hymn was 'The Day Thou Gavest, Lord, is Ended'. It has not looked back and has since the 1980s consistently been voted number 1, 2 or 3 in the BBC *Songs of Praise* polls.

Queen Victoria must have felt deeply its final words: 'So be it, Lord', the hymn concludes:

. . . thy throne shall never,
Like earth's proud empires, pass away;
Thy kingdom stands, and grows for ever,
Till all thy creatures own thy sway.

She of course ruled Britain during a time when the Christian church was taking the gospel to the far reaches of the world. 'The Day Thou Gavest', though it is also perfectly formed for morning and evening services, was actually written by John Ellerton in 1870 with these stalwart missionaries in mind. And if you follow the flow of its verses, this hymn does go out into the world like them; it begins and ends among the singers in the church congregation at home; in between, it rolls like the earth and goes with these Christian travellers into the light of other places and time spaces, where folk of other nations are praising God. And it is at the same time a hymn that reflects upon the flow of life itself.

Born in Clerkenwell John Ellerton was educated on the Isle of Man and at Trinity College, Cambridge where he came to be influenced by the founder of Christian Socialism F. D. Maurice (1805–1872). Maurice saw the Christian and social-ist philosophies as being interrelated and was in some ways a man before his time. He was a social reformer with radical ideas about the education of men and women and was loved and disliked in more or less equal measure. Charles Kingsley found him 'the most beautiful human soul whom God has ever allowed me to meet with'. John Ruskin on the other hand described Maurice as 'by nature puzzle-headed and indeed wrong headed' and Thomas Carlyle was much of the same view. John Ellerton took Holy Orders in 1850 and his inter-est in Maurice's form of Christian Socialism went hand in hand with a strong career in the church. During his final illness, the honorary title of Canon of St Albans Cathedral was given to him. At the same time, like Maurice, he devoted his energies to education. He organized, for instance, an education committee for railway workers in Crewe Green in Cheshire where he was vicar, he taught classes in English and Bible Studies, and organized one of the first Choral Associations to be established in the Midlands.

Today, John Ellerton is best known as a hymnologist – he wrote over fifty hymns in total. His talent as hymnwriter is delightfully summed up by John Julian in his monumental *Dictionary of Hymnology*: 'He weaves his moral into his metaphor, and pleases the imagination and refreshes the spirit together . . . and taken as a whole his verse is elevated in tone, devotional in spirit, and elegant in diction.'

The preferred tune for 'The Day Thou Gavest, Lord, is Ended' is 'St Clement'. This tune is said to have been written by Reverend Clement Scholefield and commissioned by his friend Arthur Sullivan – who makes quite a frequent appearance in this book – for *Church Hymns and Tunes* (1874). There have been suggestions though that Arthur Sullivan actually composed this melody. Clement Scholefield had no formal music training and between 1867 and 1872, Sullivan was organist and Clement Scholefield curate at St Peter Church in Cranley Gardens, London. It is possible that they wrote it together, and Sullivan, known for his generosity, gave the credit to his friend.*

Differences about this tune don't end here – it has been criticized for too much sentiment or for its one two three waltz-time structure and has been dropped from various editions of official hymn collections. In the *English Hymnal* of 1906, Ralph Vaughan Williams relegated it to the Appendix, known in the trade as the 'chamber of horrors'. But many perceive craftsmanship and melodic beauty in this tune, and church congregations and choirs have voted with their voices as well as for successive *Songs of Praise* polls to make this hymn one of the most loved in the last hundred years. I personally adore the sentimentality of this hymn. The undulating musical phrases are a perfect joy to sing. It is beautifully crafted musically. And I really like the idea that this is used in an evening service when we will have hopefully made the most of the day given to us by God.

* Ian Bradley, *The Daily Telegraph Book of Hymns*, 2005.

9

PRAISE MY SOUL
THE KING OF HEAVEN

Words: Henry Francis Lyte (1793–1847)
Music: John Goss (1800–80)

Praise, my soul, the King of heaven;
To his feet thy tribute bring.
Ransomed, healed, restored, forgiven,
Who like me his praise should sing?
Praise him! Praise him!
Praise the everlasting King!

Praise him for his grace and favour
To our fathers in distress;
Praise him, still the same for ever,
Slow to chide and swift to bless.
Praise him! Praise him!
Glorious in his faithfulness.

Father-like, he tends and spares us;
Well our feeble frame he knows;
In his hands he gently bears us,
Rescues us from all our foes.
Praise him! Praise him!
Widely as his mercy flows.

Angels, help us to adore him.
Ye behold him face to face;
Sun and moon, bow down before him,
Dwellers all in time and space.
Praise him! Praise him!
Praise with us the God of grace!

SOME SAY that the Book of Psalms is the only religious songbook authorised by God himself. It's certainly true that these Old Testament songs have inspired and informed hymnwriters right through the history of church music. Henry Francis Lyte chose Psalm 103 as the ground on which to build his hymn 'Praise My Soul the King of Heaven'. He captures the meaning of this psalm and honours its spirit, while in the terminology, 'paraphrasing' it. Verses 3–4 of Psalm 103, for example, give praise to the God 'Who forgiveth all thine iniquities; who healeth all thy diseases; Who redeemeth thy life from destruction; who crowneth thee with loving kindness and tender mercies'. This wonderful flow of words becomes the terrifically straightforward single line 'Ransomed, healed, restored, forgiven' in Lyte's work. Similarly, verses 8–9: 'The Lord is merciful and gracious, slow to anger, and plenteous in mercy. He will not always chide: neither will he keep his anger forever', Lyte distills into 'Slow to chide and swift to bless.'

I will talk elsewhere in this book about how Lyte's inspiration for his hymn 'Abide With Me' came from direct experience at the bedside of a dying friend. He wrote 'Praise My Soul the King of Heaven' for his Brixham parishioners fourteen years later and published it in his *The Spirit of the*

Psalms in 1834. Although this hymn is considered to be a direct paraphrase of a single psalm, perhaps like 'Abide With Me' it drew also on painful episodes in his life and is stronger for it. Henry Francis had to cope with the loss of both parents when he was a boy. His father Thomas had walked out on his family; his mother Anna then moved to London, where she died. Lyte himself was burdened by poor health through his life. These experiences could have had some bearing on one of the great themes of this hymn, how God knows and cares for us.

When Lyte lost his mother, his headmaster at Portora School in Enniskillen took over responsibility for the boy. Lyte won a scholarship to Trinity College, Dublin where he was known as a brilliant but modest scholar, winning the Prize for English Verse on three consecutive years.

This is definitely not a frothy, sentimental hymn, it's a very powerful one. I like it so much I had it sung at my wedding. I hadn't realized at the time that also the Queen had it played at her wedding to Prince Philip. It was one of the first hymns I heard sung by a congregation when I came to present *Songs of Praise* and I'll never forget the feeling it gave me hearing this powerful, uplifting hymn sung by a congregation of a thousand people. I'd shied away from hymns and from religion to a degree during my time at college and only came back to it slowly through presenting *Songs of Praise*. This hymn almost instantly bridged the gap between God and myself. When you sing it, you can't help but feel the blood pumping round your veins, such is its extreme power. It's a supernatural hymn.

I love the positive aspect of this hymn as well, especially the second verse:

'Father-like he tends and spares us / Well our feeble frame

he knows / In his hands he gently bears us / Rescues us from all our foes / Praise him praise him'. It's so reassuring to know that in the good and bad God is there with you, to hopefully guide you to better times. Singing this hymn, I feel, can change a person's mood. It's almost impossible to not get gathered up in the hymn's positive and glorifying nature.

Even though one of Lyte's lines has been changed for *Hymns Ancient and Modern* to 'Saints triumphant bow before him / Gathered in from every race', I have to say that I am still a fan of giving Christ power over the cosmos in the line 'Sun and moon bow down before him'. I think it works beautifully within the hymn. I don't think Lyte could write anything but powerful words.

And the melody, written especially for this hymn by Sir John Goss, you can tell was composed by an organist and an organist at St Paul's Cathedral, one of the greatest cathedrals this country has. It's perfect, the music really does fit with the words and it gives it that feeling of grandeur.

I've often been at church or cathedral services where you can see the congregation – how can I say this – nodding off slightly. It takes one person to yawn and the next person starts rubbing their eyes and thoughts start wandering towards Sunday lunch and what they're going to do with the rest of the day. But the minute the organ starts on 'Praise My Soul the King of Heaven' you have to up your game a little. We're asked to praise God with all that we have, our whole body and soul. The words and melody basically make us take our eyes off the world and direct them exclusively on God – and why not when He's obviously inspired this awesome piece of writing.

The primary message of the hymn is 'Praise Him, Praise

Him'. Some people will think that this repetition isn't necessary, and detracts from the rest of the writing, but I totally disagree. It reinforces the fact that we should praise God for He's the reason why we live on this earth. If it's half-hearted worship that you're after, then don't ever program this hymn into your church services, because this requires one hundred per cent praise.

10

BE STILL, MY SOUL

Words: Katharina von Schlegel (1697– c.1768)
Translation: Jane Laurie Borthwick (1813–97)
Music: Jean Sibelius (1865–1957): *Finlandia*

Be still, my soul, the Lord is on thy side,
Bear patiently the cross of grief or pain,
Leave to thy God to order and provide,
In every change he faithful will remain.
Be still, my soul, thy best, thy heavenly Friend
Through thorny ways leads to a joyful end.

Be still, my soul, thy God doth undertake
To guide the future as he has the past.
Thy hope, thy confidence let nothing shake,
All now mysterious shall be bright at last,
Be still, my soul, the waves and winds still know
His voice who ruled them while he dwelt below.

Be still, my soul: when dearest friends depart,
And all is darkened in the vale of tears,
Then shalt thou better know His love, His heart,
Who comes to soothe thy sorrow and thy fears.
Be still, my soul, thy Jesus can repay,
From his own fullness, all he takes away.

Be still, my soul, the hour is hastening on
When we shall be forever with the Lord,
When disappointment, grief and fear are gone,
Sorrow forgot, love's purest joys restored.
Be still, my soul, when change and tears are past,
All safe and blessèd we shall meet at last.

WE HAVE THE WORDS of 'Be Still, My Soul' thanks to the combined talents of two very different women who lived a century apart, and the music thanks to a great Finnish composer. I like the idea that God used three people with three different languages to give us this wonderful example of Christian patience.

There's tantalisingly little known about Katharina von Schlegel's life. She wrote down this hymn in 1752, drawing from the Psalms the reference, 'Be still, and know that I am God; I will be exalted among the nations, I will be exalted in the earth.' (Psalm 46.10.)

Katharina lived in Kothen and may have been a canoness of an evangelical women's seminary in that central German city. From an aristocratic background, she was an outstanding figure of the revival of spiritual evangelism in Germany, known as Pietism, which resembles the Puritan and Wesleyan movements in England. Spiritual revivals have often gone hand in hand with outbursts of song and though the leader of this new movement, pastor Philipp Jakob Spener (1635–1705), was not a noted hymn writer himself, his unashamed encouragement of congregational singing gave birth to this great German revival of hymns characterised by piety and faithfulness in the word of God.

A century later, in 1855, Jane Laurie Borthwick sat down to translate Katharina von Schlegel's words. The elder daughter of the manager of the North British Insurance Company in Edinburgh, Jane was a devout and active member of the Free Church of Scotland, supporter of missions abroad and social worker in her home city. She and her sister Sarah Findlater brought together their translations of German hymns into *Hymns from the Land of Luther* (published in four parts in 1854, 1855, 1858, and 1862). Jane's translation of 'Be Still' was one of these, with this note attached: 'In your patience possess ye your souls.' (Luke 21.19.) The last two lines of her translation of the second verse recall Mark 4.41: 'What manner of man is this, that even the wind and the sea obey him?'

The hymn is sung today to a melody borrowed from Jean Sibelius' symphonic poem *Finlandia*. Sibelius was born in Finland and spent most of his life there, making his home with his wife Aino and their six daughters on Lake Tuusula. He was a nationalist and a Romantic, whose work is imbued with his love of the landscape around him and its moods. His long life spanned the nineteenth and twentieth centuries. In some ways *Finlandia*, written in 1899, is a surprising source for the reflective words of this hymn; *Finlandia* was composed for a protest against Russian censorship and represents Finland's national resistance to Russia's advancing empire. However, 'Be Still, My Soul' has since 1933 been set to the serene *Finlandia Hymn* drawn from this otherwise turbulent work and later reworked by Sibelius into a stand-alone piece with words by Veikko Antero Koskenniemi.

In the twentieth century, 'Be Still, My Soul' came to be associated with another act of resistance. It was the favourite hymn of the 'Flying Scotsman' Eric Liddell, the athlete who became famous in the 1924 Olympics and again in the 1981 Academy Award-winning film *Chariots of Fire*, for refusing to run on the Sabbath. Liddell became a missionary in China, and was imprisoned during the Second World War. This hymn is an expression of total trust in God; that whatever negativity life throws in your way – salvation will prevail. In this spirit, Liddell is said to have taught it to his companions in the prison camp, where he died of a brain tumour in 1945 – shortly before the camp was liberated.

I only came to know and love this hymn through my work presenting *Songs of Praise*. Over time I have gained so much strength and comfort from the words. During my eight or so years on the show I have witnessed many memorable performances, including a very moving programme commemorating Holocaust Memorial Day, featuring the awe-inspiring voices of boy band Libera.

This hymn only became part of my repertoire very recently but it has instantly become one of those songs that I couldn't do without. It has affected me and helped me on a personal level many times. None more so than in 2008 in the North of England.

I was in Hexham Abbey in Northumberland filming *Songs of Praise* and I had been asked by the director to also record this hymn for the programme. The morning of the recording I received terrible news that a dear friend had died: the Welsh Rugby legend Ray Gravell. He was a maverick, a kind-hearted Welshman through and through and someone I cared for deeply. His death was totally unexpected as I had only spoken to him the previous day and he had seemed as always 'full of beans'. He was a young man taken well before his time.

I will never forget singing this hymn that morning – with my eyes full of tears. I had suffered a bitter loss of a friend's life and out of nowhere I felt God's presence guiding me, almost holding my hand as I sang:

> Be still, my soul: when dearest friends depart,
> And all is darkened in the vale of tears,
> Then shalt thou better know His love, His heart,
> Who comes to soothe thy sorrow and thy fears.

There I was grieving and facing up to my own mortality when the third verse dramatically builds to this:

> Be still, my soul, the hour is hastening on
> When we shall be forever with the Lord,
> When disappointment, grief, and fear are gone,
> Sorrow forgot, love's purest joys restored.
> Be still, my soul, when change and tears are past,
> All safe and blessèd we shall meet at last.

It was an intense moment – I felt that all was not lost, that Ray and myself would share a laugh and a pint again. It was only a matter of time.

Since then this hymn has followed me on my travels around the world and it never ceases to amaze me how powerful it is. Wherever I am on stage, as I stare out into the darkness of the auditorium I feel God's love and power envelope me. I hope the audience feel it too. As far as I'm concerned it's three-and-a-half minutes of magic!

11

CALON LÂN

Words: Daniel James (1848–1920)
Music: John Hughes (1872–1914)

Nid wy'n gofyn bywyd moethus,
Aur y byd na'i berlau mân:
Gofyn 'rwyf am galon hapus,
Calon onest, calon lân.

Calon lân yn llawn daioni,
Tecach yw na'r lili dlos:
Dim ond calon lân all ganu
Canu'r dydd a chanu'r nos.

Pe dymunwn olud bydol,
Hedyn buan ganddo sydd;
Golud calon lân, rinweddol,
Yn dwyn bythol elw fydd.

Chorus

Hwyr a bore fy nymuniad
Gwyd i'r nef ar adain cân
Ar i Dduw, er mwyn fy Ngheidwad,
Roddi i mi galon lân.

Chorus

H AVE YOU EVER been to a Welsh rugby match? If you
have, then you'll have been introduced to this great
Welsh hymn. It's the second anthem of Wales. It's not one to
be confined to a church or chapel, it belongs to the Nation and
that's why it's sung before, during and after Wales Rugby
Union matches. I've even sung it in those circumstances
myself, many times. Let me tell you, it fills your soul with
passion.

In 2007 it was one of the traditional Welsh hymns to be
featured on the Welsh TV channel S4C in a series called *Codi
Canu*. This was an attempt to bring choral harmony back to
the Welsh rugby terraces. This hymn is all to do with the Welsh
character and the fabric of Wales. It's our calling card if you
like. What's more important is that when the Welsh rugby
team hear it sung during a match, it really does spur them on
to greatness. It's a sort of musical tonic.

The words were written in the 1800s by Daniel James. He
came from Treboeth in Swansea and was almost entirely self-
taught, leaving school aged thirteen, and working most of his
adult life in the ironworks of the Lower Swansea Valley, for
much of it a skilled 'puddler'. His father died when he was
still quite young. As a result he used his wages to support his
mother. He also had an acknowledged poetic gift and under
his bardic name Gwyrosydd, 'Truth Will Stand', he wrote lots
of verse and some hymns too.

As a young man it is said that he was often to be found
sitting on a weird high chair in the snug of his local pub, The
King's Head, composing verse for the friends who bought him
drinks. Writing poems for pints became routine. His love of
alcohol damaged his reputation somewhat and he was known
as the 'bad boy of the chapel'. Several stories exist about his

antics – one being that he had arrived home drunk on a Saturday night only for his long-suffering wife to ban him from entering the house. Daniel went and slept the night in the pigsty. On Sunday morning he was woken by the hearty singing coming from the chapel next door. He noticed that they weren't singing a traditional 'Amen' to end the hymn. He immediately composed the poem 'Ble Mae'r Amen', which means 'Where's the Amen'.

There are more stories too – again involving his poor first wife. She apparently gave him money to buy butter. Daniel found it impossible to pass the pub and spent the cash. Afraid to go home with no butter he called at a friend's house and he borrowed some money and the next day the friend was given his reward, a skilfully written poem of thanks. His first poetry book was published when he was thrity-seven years old.

His life was far from dull – he had at least five children and became a widower by the age of forty. He married again less than a year after losing his first wife. His new wife, Gwenllian Parry, was herself a widow with five children of her own. Together they had more children. But Gwenllian died soon after the birth of their third child.

His work became more well known but never brought him tremendous wealth. He was quite prolific and more of his works were published in collections, in periodicals and news-papers. He died on 16 March 1920 a very poor man, but 'Calon Lân' is his lasting memorial – in its music setting by John Hughes. He was born near Cardigan and like Daniel suffered great hardship in his life. He worked at the Duffryn steel works near Swansea. Legend has it that he composed the tune and liked it so much he hurriedly asked Daniel to write the words to it, which he duly did, and the rest as they say is history.

There are certain words in the Welsh language that are difficult to translate and on first inspection 'Calon Lân' seems straightforward – a clean heart. However I believe the word '(g)lân' is this hymn means more. It means pure or holy.

The title of the hymn 'Calon Lân' is something I suppose we all aspire to, which is a good heart. The hymn's first lines are: 'I don't ask for a luxurious life, the world's gold or its fine pearls / I ask for a happy heart, an honest heart, a pure heart / A pure heart full of goodness is fairer than the pretty lily / none but a pure heart can sing / Sing in the day, sing in the night.'

It's typically a Welsh anthemic hymn that's been performed by almost every well-known Welsh singer, including Bryn Terfel, Katherine Jenkins, myself, a variety of male voice choirs, and recently Cerys Matthews, formerly of Catatonia. You'd not really expect her to be singing hymns, but she performed it with the Fron Male Voice Choir – to great effect. I play it often on *Good Morning Sunday* too and it always goes down very well. I strongly believe that you have to be Welsh to be able to put the heart into this piece and give it the passion it deserves and that is why it's virtually always sung in the Welsh language. Long may it continue to drive the Welsh rugby union team to achieve greatness.

12

BE THOU MY VISION

Words: Eighth-century Irish poem 'Rob tu mo bhiole,
a Comdi cride'
Translation: from the Gaelic by Mary Byrne (1880–1931)
Versified: Eleanor Hull (1860–1935)
Music: Irish folk song, *Slane*.
Other words: Joyce Torrens (1901–53) under the name Jan Struther

Be thou my vision, O Lord of my heart,
Naught be all else to me save that thou art;
Be thou my best thought in the day and the night,
Waking or sleeping thy presence my light.

Be thou my wisdom, be thou my true word,
Be thou ever with me and I with thee, Lord;
Be thou my great Father, and I thy true son;
Be thou in me dwelling, and I with thee one.

Be thou my breastplate, my sword for the fight;
Be thou my whole armour, be thou my true might;
Be thou my soul's shelter, be thou my strong tower:
Raise thou me heavenward, O Power of my power.

Riches I heed not, nor man's empty praise;
Be thou my inheritance, now and always;
Be thou and thou only the first in my heart:
O Sovereign of heaven, my treasure thou art.

High king of heaven, thou heaven's bright Sun,
O grant me its joys after victory is won;
Great Heart of my own heart, whatever befall,
Still be thou my vision, O Ruler of all.

F OR THE FIRST TIME in this book it's the melody of this
hymn that is paramount to me – I enjoy singing it to the
two sets of words, both equally as good.

The Royal Irish Academy Library in Dublin holds an eighth-
century Irish manuscript containing the pearl that is the ancient
Celtic hymn – 'Be Thou My Vision'. It needed an expert in the
language, Mary Byrne, to translate it (in 1905) and a scholar of
Old Irish to put it into verse. This was her contemporary
Eleanor Henrietta Hull, a journalist, author of such books as *A
History of Ireland and her People* and *The Poem-Book of the Gael* –
where the verses were first published in 1912 – and co-founder
and long-time Honorary Secretary of the Irish Texts Society for
the Publication of Early Manuscripts. The hymn itself first
appeared in the *Irish Church Hymnal*, 1919.

The music for 'Be Thou My Vision' is also very old; it is the
Irish folk song *Slane*, whose author may have been the saint
and martyr Dallan Forgaill (*c.* 530–598 AD). This Irish
Christian poet is said to have studied so hard that he became
blind. He was a martyr, beheaded by pirates in Donegal,
though tradition has it that God re-joined his head to his body.
He is buried there in the monastery of Inniskeel.

Both the music and original words of 'Be Thou My Vision'
were written during a period of uncertainty and warring clans
in Ireland. The hymn vividly reflects this time of insecurity,
particularly in the third verse, where it's asked of God:

Be thou my breastplate, my sword for the fight;
Be thou my whole armour, be thou my true might;
Be thou my soul's shelter, be thou my strong tower:
Raise thou me heavenward, O Power of my power.

So strong is the music of *Slane* that at least two other hymns have been set to it: 'Lord of All Hopefulness' and 'Lord of Creation'.

Slane Hill is about ten miles from Tara in County Meath. It was on Slane Hill around 433 AD that St Patrick defied a royal edict by lighting candles on Easter Eve. High King Logaire of Tara had decreed that no one could light a fire before Logaire began the pagan spring festival by lighting a fire on Tara Hill. Logaire was so impressed by Patrick's devotion that, despite his disobedience, he let him continue his missionary work. Not so surprisingly, this popular and powerful Irish hymn is often sung on 17 March, St Patrick's Day.

With its sincere words and achingly beautiful melody, 'Be Thou My Vision' has become a very popular hymn in the last fifty years or so, widely chosen as a school anthem and interestingly, although written as a Catholic hymn, it is now sung in Protestant churches throughout the world.

It has also been performed by a whole range of artists. Van Morrison recorded the hymn on his 1991 double album *Hymns to the Silence*. In 1999, it was on Seattle indie rock band Pedro the Lion's second EP and in the same year, Celtic musician Moya Brennan (Maire Brennan) sang 'Bi Thusa Mo Shuile' on her *Whisper to the Wild Water* album. One of my favourite versions is performed by the boy band Libera.

It is a fantastic hymn to sing, if a little vocally challenging because of its range. Melodically, my favourite phrases are the third and fourth ones – because of their lilting quality. I think that through the repetition of the words 'Be thou' in all verses it personalizes God – making Him a real person we really want in our lives. Even though the words are from a different age they are still very relevant to the modern Christian heart.

I have to own up here to actually also really enjoying the 'other' words that are sung to the tune *Slane* almost as much as the originals. 'Lord of All Hopefulness' was written by Joyce Torrens (1901–53), who wrote under the name of Jan Struther.

This hymn was written in 1929 at the request of Joyce Torrens' London neighbour, Canon Percy Dearmer of Westminster Abbey, for his new edition of *Songs of Praise*.

Dearmer was delighted by its triumph, announcing in *Songs of Praise Discussed* (1933) that he was 'lately returned from a service of university students, who have speedily made it their favourite'.

Torrens herself only had a small interest in Christianity, yet she managed to write very positive, forward-thinking words that are so heartfelt and touching. She takes us on a journey with God over a whole day and night. Listing His many talents and prayerfully asking for His presence at all times. My particular favourite verses are the first and last:

> Lord of all hopefulness, Lord of all joy,
> Whose trust, ever childlike, no cares could destroy,
> Be there at our waking, and give us, we pray,
> Your bliss in our hearts, Lord,
> At the break of the day.

I love the idea of waking up and having nothing but 'bliss in our hearts'. And then as a busy day eventually comes to an end:

Lord of all gentleness, Lord of all calm,
Whose voice is contentment, whose presence is balm,
Be there at our sleeping, and give us, we pray,
Your peace in our hearts, Lord,
At the end of the day.

It's no surprise that the great British nation voted 'Be Thou My Vision' as their fourth favourite hymn in a *Songs of Praise* poll. But I wonder if people were voting for the tune *Slane*, not really having a preference what words were attached to it. If a perfect hymn is the marriage of sublime lyrics with a beautiful melody then this musical masterpiece deserves its ranking position with either set of words in my book.

13

LEAD KINDLY LIGHT

Words: John Henry Newman (1801–90)
Music: John Bacchus Dykes (1823–76): *Lux Benigna*
William Henry Harris (188–1973): *Alberta*
David Evans (1874–1948): *Bonifacio*
Charles H. Purday (1799–1885): *Sandon*

Lead, kindly Light, amid the encircling gloom,
Lead thou me on;
The night is dark, and I am far from home,
Lead thou me on.
Keep thou my feet; I do not ask to see
The distant scene; one step enough for me.

I was not ever thus, nor prayed that thou
Should'st lead me on;
I loved to choose and see my path; but now
Lead thou me on.
I loved the garish day, and, spite of fears,
Pride ruled my will: remember not past years.

So long thy power hath blest me, sure it still
Will lead me on,
O'er moor and fen, o'er crag and torrent, till
The night is gone,
And with the morn those angel faces smile,
Which I have loved long since, and lost awhile.

A CELEBRATED – and controversial – Victorian wrote the poem on which 'Lead Kindly Light' is based. His influence on Christian thinking is still felt today. Queen Victoria loved John Henry Newman's poem 'The Pillar of the Cloud'; she was in two minds about its author and his religious ideas, still, on her deathbed this was the work she wanted to have read to her.

Newman experienced two conversions. His first in 1816, described as a transformation in his religious life, followed an illness when he was at private school in Ealing. 'I know perfectly well,' he wrote, 'and thankfully confess to Thee, O my God, that Thy wonderful grace turned me right round when I was more like a devil than a wicked boy, at the age of fifteen.' The 'wicked boy', rather the shy, vigorous seeker, went to Trinity College, Oxford and on to be a Fellow at Oriel, and in 1829, a year following the death of Mary, his greatly loved youngest sister, he became Vicar at St Mary's, Oxford. His search for spiritual truth continued, through his work in the Oxford Movement, as writer, thinker, preacher – and later following his second conversion and reception into the Catholic Church in 1845.

Newman wrote 'The Pillar of the Cloud' long before, in June 1833, on board a boat carrying oranges to the port of Marseilles. In *Apologia Pro Vita Sua* (1864), Newman's defence of his early thinking, he describes these events. Still suffering from a deep fever contracted in Sicily during his travels around the Mediterranean, he was enduring, nineteenth-century style, a long journey without timetables or maps. The boat became becalmed, windless, for a week in the Straits of Bonifacio. Newman was sick in body and heart. The Revolution in France, politics and Church matters in England had taken their toll on him. John Julian, author of the great *Dictionary of Hymnology*, describes the troubled state he was in as boat-bound he wrote this poem: '. . . passionately longing for home and the converse of friends; sick in body to prostration, and, as some around him feared, even unto death; feeling that he should not die but live, and that he must work, but knowing not what that work was to be, how it was to the done, or what it might tend, he breathed forth the impassioned and pathetic prayer.'

The words of that impassioned prayer are wonderful for the singer to perform. They're very descriptive words, which need almost literally to be spat out, with 'O'er moor and fen / o'er crag and torrent / till the night is gone'. You must bring out the drama of this hymn, so that it becomes almost a mini-opera. 'Lead Kindly Light' is definitely a 'slow burning' hymn. It grabs one's attention from the very first words and in the second verse the drama intensifies: 'I was not ever thus / nor prayed that thou / Should'st lead me on'. For me the high-light is the third verse: 'So long thy power hast blest me / sure it still / Will lead me on'. With those words 'still' and 'will', it's almost as if you must reinforce the message that God is there with us all the time and then 'And with the morn those angel faces smile / Which I have loved long since / and lost awhile' is a tender moment in a hymn that is quite rigorous in its word construction.

It's fair to say that there's been much conjecture about the meaning of these angel faces. Newman himself evaded clarifi-cation. He believed poetry to be 'an art which is the expres-sion not of truth, but of imagination and sentiment', and gives us the freedom to interpret for ourselves these lovely lines. The message I find in that final verse is that if you lose sight of where you are those angels are there to help you.

Newman's poem was published in *The British Magazine* of March 1834, ten years on from his ordination as an Anglican clergyman. Then, in 1836, it appeared in *Lyra Apostolica,* a collection of poems by Newman and others, where Newman added this epigraph: 'Unto the godly there ariseth up light in the darkness'.

As J. R. Watson points out*, the irregular metre of Newman's poem doesn't make for an easy transition from poem to hymn; nevertheless, it has been set to several tunes.

In the nineteenth century, Yorkshireman John Bacchus Dykes – who also set Newman's 'Praise to the Holiest in the Height' to music, composed *Lux Benigna* for the hymn and it was published in *Hymns Ancient and Modern* in 1868. Newman generously said that it was the tune that made his hymn a success: 'But you see it is not the Hymn,' he argued, 'but the *Tune,* that has gained the popularity! The Tune is Dykes', and Dr Dykes was a great Master.'

In the twentieth century, there is the 1927 setting to the tune *Bonifacio*, by David Evans, who was music editor of the *Church Hymnary*. Also, the 1931 enlarged edition of *Songs of Praise* features the setting to *Alberta* by William Henry Harris (supposedly composed on a train crossing Canada in 1924). As well as being a composer and conductor, Harris had prodigious experience as an organist, including thirty-four years as Professor of Organ and Harmony at the Royal College of Music in London and the position of organist at St George's Chapel, Windsor. He conducted at the 1937 coronation service of George VI and again at his daughter Elizabeth's coronation in 1953.

An Annotated Anthology of Hymns edited with commentary by J.R.Watson

This hymn was introduced to me by Robert Prizeman, who is the music supervisor of *Songs of Praise*, and in my view a genius when it comes to sacred music. The melody I sang it to was not John Bacchus Dykes' *Lux Benigna*, though this version is still popular, but to Charles H. Purday's *Sandon*. Purday was conductor of Psalmody at the Crown Court Scot's Church in Covent Garden in London in the 1840s, during the ministry of Dr John Cumming, whose church was so popular it was said that the traffic could not move along Bow Street or Drury Lane for the throng of carriages making their way to his services. How times have changed! Purday was a noted singer and had sung at the coronation of Queen Victoria. He became a music publisher later on in his life and was a pioneer in the movement for copyright law reform. His tune compliments beautifully John Henry Newman's words.

During my time appearing on BBC1's Saturday night entertainment show *Strictly Come Dancing*, I happened also to be on tour in Britain. It was the largest tour I had ever undertaken. Three or four months earlier, I had come across a Status Quo poster announcing their largest ever tour in Britain, with something like 45 dates involved. I turned round to my colleague – who happened also to be the concert promoter – and half in jest said that I wanted to do a bigger tour. So we embarked on a mammoth tour while I was on *Strictly*, which was, looking back, utter madness. Every evening, up and down Scotland, Ireland, Wales and England there was not a hall I didn't go to – at least it felt that way. During the day I would rehearse dances that were totally alien to me and then in the evening I would be on familiar territory – on the concert platform. So the day was filled with sequins and punchy rhythms and many blisters and teary moments and the

night totally the opposite. I'd open the concert in total darkness, singing unaccompanied the first verse of 'Lead Kindly
Light'. It was extraordinary gauging audiences' experience of
this because I don't think anyone had started a concert tour
unaccompanied before. All that could be heard at first was my
voice off stage singing the hymn. Then as the introduction to
the second verse began, I would walk out onto the platform.
These concerts started with no lights, no gimmicks, nothing,
just the first verse of 'Lead Kindly Light', which offers some
of the hymn's most powerful words: 'Lead, kindly light, amid
the encircling gloom / Lead thou me on / The night is dark
and I am far from home / Lead thou me on / Keep thou my
feet; I do not ask to see / The distant scene; one step enough
for me'. From this simple start, people gave their concentrat-
ed attention for the next hour and a half. What I try to do with
my singing is to take people on a musical journey. Here I was
beginning the evening stripped of everything but the voice
and building layer upon layer, with organ, then strings, then
harp, then guitar. You can really do that with this hymn.

When I started that first verse offstage, I was away from
home and the night was midwinter dark. Opening with
'Lead Kindly Light' was the ideal way for me to ask for God's
help in the following two hours, where I was performing
to an audience of anything from a thousand to two thousand
people. It was up to me to give of my best, but if I needed that
helping hand, I knew it would be there.

14

ANGEL VOICES, EVER SINGING

Words: Francis Pott 1832–1909
Music: E. G. Monk 1819–1900

Angel voices, ever singing
Round Thy throne of light,
Angel harps, forever ringing,
Rest not day or night;
Thousands only live to bless Thee
And confess Thee
Lord of might.

Thou who art beyond the farthest
Mortal eye can scan,
Can it be that Thou regardest
Songs of sinful man?
Can we know that Thou art near us
And wilt hear us?
Yea, we can.

Yea, we know that Thou rejoicest
O'er each work of Thine;
Thou didst ears and hands and voices
For Thy praise design;
Craftsman's art and music's measure
For Thy pleasure
All combine.

In Thy house, great God, we offer
Of Thine own to Thee;
And for Thine acceptance proffer,
All unworthily,
Hearts and minds and hands and voices
In our choicest
Psalmody.

Honour, glory, might and merit,
Thine shall ever be,
Father, Son and Holy Spirit,
Blessed Trinity!
Of the best that Thou hast given
Earth and heaven
Render Thee.

'Hearts and minds and hands and voices / In our choicest Psalmody' – a great tribute to the joy of lifting up our voices in song.

'Angel Voices, Ever Singing' was written and composed to mark the establishment of a new organ in a Lancashire church. William Macrorie, Dean of St John the Evangelist at Wingates, asked his friend Francis Pott to write a hymn for the occasion. Pott's verses, set to the music of Dr Edwin Monk, really capture the delight of singing with the organ to the glory of God: 'Thou didst ears and hands and voices for Thy praise design / Craftsman's art and music's measure for Thy pleasure all combine.'

Francis Pott was best known as a translator of hymns, who edited hymnals and contributed to *Hymns Ancient and Modern* (1861). He apparently did not rate his own compositions highly, claiming that there was nothing interesting to say about them. But 'Angel Voices' is evidence to the contrary; it is an original work and catches beautifully the actual and special experience of standing up together in church and singing hymns.

This hymn tune is also one of Edwin George Monk's finest. As well as being a notable organist, he composed many hymns, choral concert works, anthems and the librettos of three oratorios. He co-founded the Oxford University Motet and Madrigal Society, was a Biblical scholar and a keen amateur astronomer – becoming a Fellow of the Royal Astronomical Society in 1871.

Composing music for a new organ must have been a task close to Edwin Monk's heart. He was organist of York Minster for twenty-four years. When he started at the Minster in 1859, an 'extraordinary' organ was in place. In 1829, a fire had been started by a 'madman' who disliked organs – it destroyed both the organ and the Quire roof. Not a pipe or a pedal of the original organ of 1634 survived. It was replaced by a new one designed by Elliott and Hill, which was completed in 1834. But the design was ill-conceived and the organ considered too heavy to play. Over the next few years frequent modifications were made, but it wasn't until 1859 that the problems were finally solved by Edwin Monk, who chose William Hill & Sons to replace the 'gargantuan horror' with an instrument of 'balanced musical character' to his own design. The organ case remained intact but new pipework was introduced. A number of these pipes remain today.

John Betjeman considered church organists to be a splendid breed of people, 'often eccentric, sometimes doctrinaire, seldom anonymous. It's hard to hide your light under a bushel when all that huge potential of sound is at your fingers – and feet.' And the members of this splendid breed have made a real contribution to the composition of church music. They include Henry John Gauntlett (1805–1876), who composed over a thousand hymns and carols, his most famous being the melody for 'Once in Royal David's City'; Sir John Goss (1810–1880), organist at St Paul's Cathedral, who wrote the tune of 'Praise my Soul the King of Heaven', and Arthur Sullivan, who also wrote a melody for 'Angel Voices', published in *The Hymnary* in 1872. He made his living for some time as church organist of St Michael's Church in Pimlico (where his adult choir members were drawn from the local police station), before going on to fame and some fortune with his operas with W. S. Gilbert. His melodies for 'Onward Christian Soldiers' and 'Nearer my God to Thee' are both acknowledged in this book.

All I have to do is see 'Angel Voices' in an order of service or begin to hear the first strains of the melody and I immediately get extreme butterflies in the pit of my stomach. It takes me back to being a nine-year-old and my very first service as a probationer at Bangor Cathedral, which in those days I thought was the largest cathedral in the world. It's only from my work on *Songs of Praise* that I realize that Bangor Cathedral is actually only a glorified church in its size. That Sunday morning I put on the purple robes for the first time – the cassock and the ruff – no surplice of course because I was still a probationer – and processed in with the choir, and the only hymn that I had to sing as a probationer was 'Angel Voices, Ever Singing'. I'll never forget the feeling of being in that building; I was in heaven and hell at the same moment. Heaven, being part of the choir I was incredibly proud of. Hell as in I really didn't want to mess it up. I was nervous, looking up at the grown-up boy choristers and the lay clerks and thinking to myself that with hard work and a bit of luck I could possibly be in the main choir one day. I sang the hymn and wasn't told off by the choirmaster, so I think I got away with it, but every time I hear this hymn now it takes me back to that moment. It think this is an absolutely beautiful melody and when I've been fortunate enough to be at a *Songs of Praise* recording, and we start singing this hymn, the mood of the whole congregation lightens. The chances are they may be tired, having sung five 'Guide Me O Thou Great Redeemer's in a row, trying to get it right, but the minute you start singing 'Angel Voices', as far as I'm concerned the soul really does shine. It's what brings out the best in a congregation and I suppose that's why it's such a fantastic hymn. There are some great lines in it. One of my favourites, the beautifully crafted 'Thou didst ears and hands and voices / For Thy praise design / Craftsman's art and music's measure / For Thy pleasure all combine'. And the final verse – you really don't get much better than 'Honour, glory, might and merit / Thine shall ever be'. It's the punctuation marks that really make it, allowing you to pronounce every word, 'honour' – 'glory' – 'might' – 'merit'. The whole rhythm of the thing gives it an impressive dignity. 'Father, Son and Holy Spirit / Blessed trinity'. It's just so majestic.

Another important aspect of 'Angel Voices' to take into account is the fact that you've got to have good breath control to sing it. It's not simply a case of breathing at the end of each line of the verse. In this hymn some of the lines are connected in thought – 'Craftsman's art and music's measure for Thy pleasure / all combine' and equally 'Thousands only live to bless Thee / And confess Thee / Lord of might' – and the highlight of that verse is the last line. I've been standing next to people singing this where the 'Lord of might' is really quite timid because they've simply run out of breath. It's not an easy song but you feel you've really achieved something if you've managed to pull it off.

I've said it before in this book but this hymn does exactly what it says on the tin: it is unadulterated praise of God.

15

MY SONG IS LOVE UNKNOWN

Words: Samuel Crossman (1624–83)
Music: John Ireland (1879–1962)

My song is love unknown,
My Savior's love to me;
Love to the loveless shown,
That they might lovely be.
O who am I,
That for my sake
My Lord should take
Frail flesh, and die?

He came from His blest throne
Salvation to bestow,
But men made strange, and none
The longed-for Christ would know.
But O, my friend,
My friend indeed,
Who at my need
His life did spend.

Sometimes they strew His way,
And His sweet praises sing,
Resounding all the day
Hosannas to their King:

Then 'Crucify!'
Is all their breath,
And for His death
They thirst and cry.

Why, what hath my Lord done?
What makes this rage and spite?
He made the lame to run,
He gave the blind their sight.
Sweet injuries!
Yet they at these
Themselves displease,
And 'gainst Him rise.

They rise, and needs will have
My dear Lord made away;
A murderer they save,
The Prince of life they slay.
Yet cheerful He
To suffering goes,
That He His foes
From thence might free.

In life, no house, no home
My Lord on earth might have;
In death, no friendly tomb,
But what a stranger gave.
What may I say?
Heav'n was His home;
But mine the tomb
Wherein He lay.

Here might I stay and sing,
No story so divine;
Never was love, dear King,
Never was grief like Thine!
This is my Friend,
In whose sweet praise
I all my days
Could gladly spend.

HERE'S ONE of those hymns – there are quite a few of them in my top forty – where the words and the music come together only after centuries have passed. It's musically also one of those where the melody seems to have come effortlessly to the composer in minutes!

Christ's passion is the theme of a number of the hymns I've chosen, including 'The Old Rugged Cross', 'There is a Green Hill Far Away', and 'When I Survey the Wondrous Cross'. Samuel Crossman's hymn for Passiontide is a quite 'literary' hymn, fully of irony, of paradox and dramatic exclamation, but it is also a personal one and its final lines simply praise God for this extraordinary event and add:

This is my friend,
In whose sweet praise
I all my days
Could gladly spend.

Samuel Crossman was an Anglican divine, who wrote religious verse 'upon select subjects and scriptures' as he put it. The Welsh poet and priest George Herbert (1593–1633), whose mother Magdalene was a friend and patron of John

Donne, was a rather daunting influence I'd imagine on Crossman's work. Herbert's collection of poems: *The Temple: Sacred Poems and Private Ejaculations* was having a strong impression on the hymn writers of the mid-seventeenth-century. The poems in *The Temple* drew their form and their meaning from church architecture and several of them became hymns, including 'Teach Me, My God and King' and 'Let All the World in Every Corner Sing'. Crossman seems to have taken to heart Herbert's observation that 'A Verse may find him whom a Sermon flies' and in 1664 wrote this poem on the Passion of Christ. He published it in a small book, more of a pamphlet, called *The Young Man's Meditation*, described by its author as 'Sacred Poems upon Select Subjects and Scriptures'.

Crossman lived during a period in the seventeenth century when Anglicans and Puritans were at loggerheads. Though an Anglican divine, Crossman was by persuasion a Puritan, and this got him expelled from his parish in the fallout from the 1662 Act of Uniformity. But Crossman recanted and spent most of the years that followed, to his death in 1683, back in the fold of the Anglican church as Dean of Bristol Cathedral.

John Ireland, whose melody for Crossman's poem made this hymn a popular favourite, set the poem to his piece 'Love Unknown' three centuries later, just after World War I. It has been said that he wrote it in ten minutes over lunch on the back of a menu! Whatever, the circumstances he did a marvellous job of it and this version of the hymn was published in 1919, in *The Public School Hymnbook*.

Ireland was born in Bowdon near Manchester, the son of a publisher and newspaper proprietor. His childhood was not an easy one, his mother died in 1893 and his father a year later

when John was only fifteen. He entered the Royal College of
Music in his teens, studied piano, organ and composition
under Charles Villiers Stanford there and went on to teach at
the College, where one of his pupils was Benjamin Britten.
His musical influences included Ravel, Debussy and
Stravinsky. He wrote some of the best songs in the English
repertoire, setting poems by Hardy, Houseman, Masefield,
Rupert Brooke and Christina Rossetti – and of course Samuel
Crossman.

John Ireland happens to be one of my favourite composers.
When I was a student at the Royal Academy of Music, it was
a pleasure to sing John Ireland's songs. In my first year at
the Academy I was way too young vocally to tackle the big
repertoire and all I could manage was English song, so I
performed lots of John Ireland and lots of music by people
like Michael Head and Roger Quilter. They gave me a First in
my examinations at the end of the first year, but one of my
assessors had written on my report that musically they
couldn't fault me and that the brain knew exactly how to sing,
but as an eighteen-year-old, my voice wasn't mature enough
for the task – except for the John Ireland piece. There seemed
to be an effortless connection between his composition and
my voice.

It suited my soul too. Being a chorister at Bangor was a
wonderful experience, but there were special moments, and I
can count them on one hand, where I felt a connection
between what I was singing and God actually being in the
place.

I remember us singing 'My Song is Love Unknown' in
Evensong services on Tuesdays and Thursdays when there
would be only one or two people in the congregation. In a

large cathedral, lit only with candlelight at dusk, and having that open space available for us to perform this song was a total pleasure. I used to particularly enjoy the lines: 'O who am I / that for my sake / My Lord should take / Frail flesh and die'. And 'But O, my friend, / My friend indeed / Who at my need / His life did spend!'.

I really love this hymn because it's not typically hymnal in its melodic construction. John Ireland really knows how to write for the singer and as far as I'm concerned, when you are performing it, musically it seems to lift you up to a higher plane. Not many pieces can do this – and I bet even less that were written on the back of a bill of fare!

16

MI GLYWAF DYNER LAIS – SARAH

Words and Music: Lewis Hartsough (1828–72)
Translation: John Roberts (1822–77)
Music: William Arnold (1768–1832)

Mi glywaf dyner lais
yn galw arnaf fi
i ddod a golchi meiau i gyd
yn afon Calfari.

Arglwydd, dyma fi
ar dy alwad di,
canna fenaid yn y gwaed
a gaed ar Galfari.

Yr Iesu syn fy ngwadd
i dderbyn gydai saint
ffydd, gobaith, cariad pur a hedd
a phob rhyw nefol fraint.

Yr Iesu syn cryfhau
om mewn ei waith drwy ras;
maen rhoddi nerth im henaid gwan
i faeddu mhechod cas.

Gogoniant byth am drefn
y cymod ar glanhad;

derbyniaf Iesu fel yr wyf
a channaf am y gwaed.

*

I hear Thy welcome voice
That calls me, Lord, to Thee,
For cleansing in Thy precious blood
That flowed on Calvary.

I am coming Lord!
Coming now to Thee!
Wash me, cleanse me in the blood
That flowed on Calvary!

Though coming weak and vile,
Thou dost my strength assure;
Thou dost my vileness fully cleanse,
Till spotless all, and pure.

'Tis Jesus calls me on
To perfect faith and love,
To perfect hope and peace and trust,
For earth and Heav'n above.

'Tis Jesus Who confirms
The blessèd work within,
By adding grace to welcomed grace,
Where reigned the power of sin.

And He the witness gives
To loyal hearts and free
That every promise is fulfilled,
If faith but brings the plea.

All hail! atoning blood!
All hail! redeeming grace!
All hail! the gift of Christ our Lord,
Our Strength and Righteousness.

THE WORDS AND MUSIC to this hymn were originally written in English by Lewis Hartsough back in 1872, with the title 'Welcome Voice'. It was translated into Welsh by John Roberts, otherwise known as Ieuan Gwyllt, which means Wild Ieuan – an interesting name really for a hymn-writer. Wild Ieuan was a prominent Calvinistic Methodist minister and a fine musician. He wrote quite a few volumes of tunes for hymns and also tonic sol far books for Wales. As I have said elsewhere in this book he was a giant as far as promotion of Welsh hymn tunes was concerned.

If you're born in Wales then you're probably aware of two different tunes for this hymn. One of them is 'Gwahoddiad', which is a translation of the English 'welcome'. It also means an invitation and is a favourite with Welsh male voice choirs the world over. It's ideal for choral singing.

The melody I mostly associate with the Welsh words is 'Sarah', which was written by William Arnold, and it's a more tender melody than Hartsough's, which roars along. It's an ethereal tune that I used to perform as an encore in my concerts as a boy soprano, unaccompanied. There's something particularly touching and sincere about the melody if you perform it that way.

There's no denying that Lewis Hartsough's words are beautifully crafted and grab you instantly: 'Mi glywaf dyner lais yn galw arnaf fi', translated are 'I hear Thy welcome voice that calls me Lord to thee/For cleansing in Thy precious blood that flowed on Calvary'. And the intensity builds as it goes along. The refrain is 'Arglwydd dyma fi, Ar dy alwad di, canna fenaid yn y gwaed a gaed ar Galfari.' – 'I am coming Lord /Coming now to Thee/Cleanse me in the blood that flowed on Calvary'. The Welsh translation of the second verse means Jesus who invites me to receive with his saints, faith, hope, pure love and peace, and every heavenly privilege. The final verse is yet again incredibly strong, meaning Jesus who strengthens me to work through grace he gives me strength to my weak soul. Beats my hateful sins. The final verse that I used to sing is 'Glory forever. All Hail I receive Jesus as I am and sing about the blood'. If it's pure theatre you're after then look no further than this hymn.

Even though I would imagine that I'm in a minority, especially as a Welshman, my favoured tune is the one by William Arnold. He worked in Her Majesty's shipyard in Portsmouth. He was also choir-master of the Daniel Street Wesleyan Church near Landport. He wrote many of his tunes whilst working in the shipyard and was known to note them down using his carpenter's pencil on a piece of board. This is how 'Sarah' was composed. Let me assure you there is nothing wooden about his melody!

I performed 'Mi Glywaf Dyner Lais' as an encore at concerts in parish church halls or larger stages when I was a child. It seemed to me an ideal way to round off an evening's concert, just one lone voice telling a powerful story. No accompaniment, no gimmicks, just heart and soul. I went out to Israel around this time to record three programmes for the BBC – two for Easter and one for Christmas. *Voices from the Holy Land* was probably the most watched programme on television of that period. To celebrate the fact that the BBC Welsh Chorus and myself were in Israel it was decided to put on a concert at the Mann Auditorium in Tel Aviv (where they'd also held the Eurovision Song Contest). It was a bittersweet experience for me because at the time the BBC couldn't afford for my mother and father to continue staying with me in Israel, so my parents had to return home to Wales, leaving me to continue with the filming for three more days. So I knew that the morning after this concert they were going and I would be staying out there with my singing teacher. I was only twelve or thirteen at the time, so this wasn't a comfortable experience. I was on stage with the BBC Welsh Symphony Chorus and the audience was clamouring, 'Go on, do another song, do another song!' but I didn't actually have up my sleeve another song to sing. The pressure of knowing that my parents were leaving the next day and performing in front of three thousand people was too much – I walked off the stage and burst into tears because I didn't know what to do. It was the only time in my career as a boy soprano when I felt that I was not in control. Needless to say, I pulled myself together, walked back on stage and instead of acknowledging the poor pianist, I went to the centre of the stage and sang without accompaniment 'Mi Glywaf Dyner Lais' – I hear thy tangential voice calling me – and thankfully it went down rather well.

I recorded 'My Glywaf Dyner Lais' on my first record as a boy soprano, in Bangor Cathedral. It was a piece I decided to record unaccompanied as well. This was a very surreal experience. To get the sound right, I sang it from the pulpit. I had never stepped into the pulpit before even though I knew my cathedral like the back of my hand. The other tracks for the disc were recorded in the choir stalls or in front of the altar. The pulpit for me as a chorister was a very Holy place where our most loved Dean Ivor Rees would deliver his very important sermons as we choristers would occasionally nod off! I felt I was letting the Dean of Bangor Cathedral down by stepping into his spot. Once I was told that the Dean had no problem with me singing from the pulpit, I could let rip! And I did!

17

JERUSALEM

Words: William Blake (1757–1827)
Music: Charles Hubert Hastings Parry (1848–1918)

And did those feet in ancient time
Walk upon England's mountains green?
And was the holy Lamb of God
On England's pleasant pastures seen?

And did the Countenance Divine
Shine forth upon our clouded hills?
And was Jerusalem builded here
Among those dark Satanic mills?

Bring me my bow of burning gold!
Bring me my arrows of desire!
Bring me my spear: O clouds, unfold!
Bring me my chariot of fire!

I will not cease from mental fight,
Nor shall my sword sleep in my hand
Till we have built Jerusalem
In England's green and pleasant land

I FIRST CAME to hear of 'Jerusalem' on my second day in David Hughes Comprehensive School in Menai Bridge on Anglesey. As an eleven-year-old I was summoned into the hall by the music teacher and much to my embarrassment, during a lunch break in front of about 200 other pupils, she explained to me that she wanted me to sing 'Jerusalem'. She'd heard that I had quite a nice voice. Now, I never thought there was anything special about my voice at all. I used to sing all the solos in primary school and I'd just joined Bangor Cathedral Choir, but I'd never sung 'Jerusalem'. So she banged through the notes on this old upright piano and I did what came naturally to me and sang it. After that I sang every solo in secondary school for the next six years.

Even as an eleven-year-old I remember being bowled over by the immense power of this hymn, that it really did stir my young soul. Those lines, 'Bring me my bow of burning gold / Bring me my chariot of fire', for instance are extraordinary writing. I've only recorded it once as an adult, which has nothing to do with the fact that it features the line 'England's green and pleasant land' and that I'm a Welshman – it doesn't . . . honestly. I have though performed 'Jerusalem' many times. Invariably, at various Last Night of the Proms concerts across Britain, invariably in pouring rain. You sing 'Land of Hope and Glory' then 'Jerusalem' then a spitfire flies past – another concert done! Obviously, this is testament to this hymn that it can be sandwiched between 'Land of Hope and Glory' and a spitfire. It's magnificent hymn-writing – words and music working as one.

William Blake is said to have perceived abstract ideas as people, or angels; he was a visionary and perhaps a fantasist, but he also had a very strong sense of the hardship, the urban desolation surrounding him in the London – and the England – of his times. London was his home; he was brought up there, and his parents ran a hosier's shop in Broad Street. They gave him an apprenticeship in engraving, he won a place at the Royal Academy Schools, and for the remainder of his life he worked as an engraver, while practising his 'propensity for writing unintelligible verse'.* He wrote an entirely intelligible short poem to introduce one of his 'Prophetic Books', *Milton*. Only four copies of *Milton* are known to exist – an engraver by trade, Blake tended to create a few individual copies of his works to sell.

Technically 'Jerusalem' isn't a hymn at all, as it isn't a prayer to God, and some vicars have apparently banned it from their services. There's much discussion about its meaning. It is generally agreed that it was inspired by a legend that Jesus came to England as a boy and established a second Jerusalem at Glastonbury, Somerset. This legend may be linked to the idea of the 'Second Coming' described in the Book of Revelation. Some people suggest that 'Jerusalem' is a metaphor for heaven, briefly created by Jesus's visit, which offers a clear contrast to the 'dark satanic mills' possibly representing the industrial revolution, the destruction of nature or even factories producing armaments for war. Another view is that 'Jerusalem' represents new humanity freed from imperialism and war, and yet another that the 'dark satanic mills' represent the Church of England's lacklustre church ceremonies, full of routine ceremony but lacking in spirituality.

As far as composer Charles Hubert Hastings Parry is concerned, if you had one piece like 'Jerusalem' on your CV,

* Peter Ackroyd, *Blake* (Sinclair-Stevenson, London, 1995)

you could be proud. But he also wrote the coronation hymn 'I Was Glad' and of course the tune 'Repton' which sets the words 'Dear Lord and Father of Mankind'. We're talking here of a serious hymn composer. Hubert Parry wrote 'Jerusalem' in the last decade of his life. By then he had resigned from Oxford, where he was Professor of Music, on his doctor's advice. He composed the music for 'Jerusalem' in 1916 after being asked by the then Poet Laureate, Robert Bridges, to do so for a patriotic anthology of verse. Before then 'Jerusalem' was a little known poem but in 1916 when there were thousands of casualties in the First World War and national morale was low it seemed to encapsulate what Britain was fighting for. In peace as well as war, sung in churches and halls, by idealists and realists, it seems to be an anthem of hope, that we can make a better society and eventually a better country.

I really like the idea that 'Jerusalem' is used to round off an evening of musical entertainment, where usually the whole community has come together. Maybe for the very first time. This reminds one of what Blake was writing about, that he doesn't make firm statements of truth in his poem. He says that there may or may not have been a divine visit, that there was briefly heaven in England. That was then, he's saying, now we're faced with the challenge of once again creating a country where heaven prevails. If that is the message and inspiration that people are taking away from a great evening's entertainment, where they've been rubbing shoulders with strangers as well as friends, then that can only be a positive thing. I have always believed that music does have the power to stir and change lives, to bring fragmented communities together; maybe this hymn is proof.

18

MORNING HAS BROKEN

Words: Eleanor Farjeon (1881–1965)
Music: Gaelic melody, *Bunessan*

Morning has broken
Like the first morning.
Blackbird has spoken
Like the first bird.
Praise for the singing,
Praise for the morning,
Praise for them, springing
Fresh from the Word.

Sweet the rain's new fall
Sunlit from heaven,
Like the first dewfall
On the first grass.
Praise for the sweetness
Of the wet garden
Sprung in completeness
Where his feet pass.

Mine is the sunlight,
Mine is the morning
Born of the one light
Eden saw play.

Praise with elation,
Praise every morning,
God's re-creation
Of the new day.

© Eleanor Farjeon, *The Children's Bells*

'MORNING HAS BROKEN', is a joyful hymn of praise, as 'fresh as the first dewfall', to be sung daily around breakfast time and in school assemblies around the western world. Fittingly it was at first light that its author Eleanor Farjeon found the words, while staying with her friend, the poet Alice Meynell, at her home in Greatham, Sussex. Farjeon had been commissioned by Percy Dearmer, one of the editors of *Songs of Praise,* to write a hymn of gratitude for and celebration of 'the new day'. This, in three short verses, is what she gave him, and he set it to the Gaelic folk melody *Bunessan.*

Eleanor Farjeon's 'Morning has Broken' is a song of innocence. As Marjorie Reeves and Jenyth Worsley put it in *Favourite Hymns*, she 'takes us in an imaginative leap right back to the very first morning in the garden of Eden before the fall, as Adam and Eve take delight in the first blackbird, the first grass, the first light.' She is best known today as a writer of books for children like the magical *Martin Pippin in the Apple Orchard* (1921) or *The Little Bookroom* (1955), and there's a direct childlike energy in this hymn.

She wrote more hymns for the 1931 *Songs of Praise*, including 'More Lovely than the Noonday Rest' and 'Fields of Corn, Give Up Your Eyes'. Her 1928 carol, 'People, Look East!' is a popular one with children's choirs.

'Nellie' Farjeon's father Benjamin was a popular novelist, her maternal grandfather an American theatrical giant, the actor Joseph Jefferson; her brothers Joseph and Herbert were writers and the eldest, Harry, was a composer (Eleanor wrote the libretto for his operetta *Floretta*). So the literary London life was her metier. She earned her living as writer of fiction, poetry, and journalism and lived and worked in the same new air as the women who, like her, were coming to literary prominence after the First World War. The writers Vera Brittain, Rose Macaulay and Mary Webb, poets Charlotte Mew and Nellie's friend Alice Meynell, were all coming into their own once that traumatic war had ended. D. H. Lawrence, Walter de la Mare and Robert Frost were Eleanor's friends and she enjoyed a close friendship with the poet Edward Thomas and his wife Helen.

Eleanor did not marry, but she had a relationship with English teacher George Earle (known as Pod) that lasted thirty years. Her interest in religion was constant through her life. She was intrigued by her contemporaries' preoccupation with spiritualism and tempted by ideas of reincarnation. On her 70th birthday in 1951, she was received into the Catholic Church.

Mary MacDonald (1789–1872), who wrote the melody that became 'Morning Has Broken', was born at Torranuach-drach, near the small village of Bunessan on the Ross of Mull. The family (she had ten children) were crofters. Mary MacDonald was also a notable Gaelic poet. She had set her poem *Leanabh an Aigh* to a traditional melody and it was translated by Lachlann MacBean for his 1888 *Songs and Hymns of the Gael* as the carol 'Child in a Manger'. It was this melody, *Bunessan* (in Gaelic *Bun-Easin*, 'foot of the little waterfall'), that Percy Dearmer was referring to when he asked Eleanor

Farjeon to write verses for this 'lovely Gaelic tune'.

It seems that the 'lovely Gaelic tune' and glorious words are enjoyed the world over. It's become very popular with recording artists. It's featured on Neil Diamond's 1992 *Christmas Album*, the Mormon Tabernacle Choir's 2003 album, *Consider the Lilies*, and other artists who have recorded it include Judy Collins, Art Garfunkel, Nana Mouskouri, and Roger Whittaker. Also, if you care to, you can find singer and actor Ellen Greene singing it in the rain as Vivien Charles in the TV series *Pushing Daisies*. I've even recorded it myself.

You wouldn't be in the minority if you thought that 'Morning Has Broken' was written by Cat Stevens and Rick Wakeman. For many many years, I actually thought the same thing. I can't listen to 'Morning Has Broken' these days without imagining Rick playing that piano accompaniment – it *makes* the piece of music. But my association with the hymn goes back to the age of six or seven when I used to take part in Eisteddfods in Wales, art competitions basically, where you performed; I couldn't recite poetry or dance, so instead I sang. I remember singing 'Morning Has Broken' in Welsh at a local Eisteddfod in one of the chapels in North Wales and it was one of the first experiences I had as a child of really enjoying being in front of an audience. Before then I used to absolutely hate performing and I always seemed to have to sing for grandparents or visitors who came to the house – I'm not quite sure why. But in this particular competition something just clicked – I was way down the list of competitors to venture onto the stage, so needless to say the congregation were fed up with hearing different versions of 'Morning Has Broken' by the time my moment to shine came about, but I got up there and gave it my all and really loved the experience. It's an extremely beautiful melody and very easy for the singer to communicate the message. It takes you on the journey without you having to force the message.

Not a week went by at Llandegfan Primary School where 'Morning Has Broken' wasn't sung in a school assembly and it seems like an obvious choice, it uplifts you to start a new day. If you're working in a factory in China, you do some Tai Chi but I tell you what, in Llandegfan Primary School, 'Morning Has Broken' did the trick, it hit the mark. 'Morning Has Broken' is the musical vitamin you take that enables you to face the trials and tribulations of the day.

I've mentioned the fact that this melody is beautiful and well-written in a very simplistic way. The words on the other hand are incredibly descriptive. You can tell instantly when you listen to them that their author was writing for children, because she gets you immediately into the story of the hymn and the adjectives that she uses really do let you know exactly what it's about. There's no hidden message in this one, it's obvious in a marvellous rejoicing way.

When my singing voice did decide finally to head south, colleagues at school used to mock me by singing to this tune 'Aled's voice has broken'. It was funny for the first playground session but after about six months, it did get a little bit tiresome!

19

ABIDE WITH ME

Words: Henry Francis Lyte (1793–1847)
Music: William Henry Monk (1823–89): *Eventide*

Abide with me; fast falls the eventide;
The darkness deepens; Lord, with me abide,
When other helpers fail, and comforts flee,
Help of the helpless, O abide with me.

Swift to its close ebbs out life's little day;
Earth's joys grow dim, its glories pass away;
Change and decay in all around I see;
O thou who changest not, abide with me.

I need thy presence every passing hour;
What but thy grace can foil the tempter's power?
Who like thyself my guide and stay can be?
Through cloud and sunshine, O abide with me.

I fear no foe with thee at hand to bless;
Ills have no weight, and tears no bitterness.
Where is death's sting? Where, grave, thy victory?
I triumph still, if thou abide with me.

Hold thou thy cross before my closing eyes;
Shine through the gloom, and point me to the skies:
Heaven's morning breaks, and earth's vain shadows flee;
In life, in death, O Lord, abide with me.

(Go on, admit it – does this hymn make you think of football?
Me too!)

THE WORDS FOR 'Abide with Me' were written by Henry
Francis Lyte, who drew inspiration from the disciples'
invitation to the risen Christ on the road to Emmaus in the
Gospel of Luke (24:29): 'Abide with us: for it is toward
evening and the day is far spent.'

Lyte was born in 1793 near Kelso in the Scottish borders.
He was educated at Trinity College, Dublin and ordained in
1815. He served from 1823 to the year of his death as
perpetual curate of the seaside Devonshire parish of Lower
Brixham, where he wrote his most celebrated hymns 'Abide
with Me' and 'Praise my Soul the King of Heaven'.

Of course the experience of the evening tide would have
been familiar to Lyte at his parish by the sea. The story goes
that the hymn came to him when as a young curate in Ireland
he attended the death bed of an old friend, whose repetition
of the phrase 'Abide with me' so struck Lyte that he wrote the
hymn around these words.

But Lyte was dogged by ill health and it was not until he
was himself close to death in 1847 that he gave to a relative a
manuscript version of the hymn following his last service at
Brixham Church.

Even though Lyte wrote his own music to the words he'd
written, it's William Henry Monk's tune *Eventide* that we all
sing. Whether the myth that Monk wrote it in ten minutes is
true, it's still musical perfection and it's almost as if the same
person wrote the words and the music because they go
together so well. Echoing Lyte's dying friend, the words
repeat quite a lot the phrase 'Abide with me,' but that just

reinforces the message that you're desperate for God to be with you in whatever you do. (Repetition – could it be the key, or one of the keys, to a hymn's success?)

'Abide With Me' is not one of my top ten favourites. Even though I've sung it many times I have to admit to finding it quite a tough song. Sustaining the long, drawn out phrases takes a lot out of you. But it has a feeling of grandeur, of power. It's not a hymn that you can rush, it's very stately and just when you think that it can't stir you any more than it has, in comes the glorious descant of the final verse. Ideal for before a big football match like the FA Cup Final, it sets the scene for what's to follow. Both teams want God on their side in order to prosper and it seems fitting that it says 'In life, in death, O Lord, abide with me' because let's face it, the FA Cup Final is just that, a life or death situation for those football players and respected fans.

When you delve back through history, it's obvious why this hymn has been with people in times of danger, or hardship, or just before death. In 1915, Edith Cavell, the English nurse shot by the Germans for aiding the flight of wounded soldiers, understood its acknowledgment of approaching death and sang it in her cell on the night before she was executed. I've been to the site of the World War I trenches and the fact that I could picture the soldiers singing 'Abide With Me' made the experience all the more poignant. It's a rather unexceptional place now, not much there, but I can't begin to imagine what it was like during war. To have this hymn and to be able to recite its words or sing its melody must have been a great comfort to the soldiers, who didn't know if it was to be life or death for them.

In September 2001, a Salvation Army band played 'Abide

With Me' at Ground Zero following the 11 September attack on the World Trade Centre. 'Abide With Me' is definitely not something that you perform lightheartedly. You have to give 100 per cent to this hymn for it to work. It's not about half singing, it's about giving it every ounce of energy you have. It's singing from the whole soul. A total hymn commitment is required. Watch this space but I'll be tackling this hymn again on record soon, and who knows, I may find the key that unlocks its magic. And, my beloved Arsenal Football Club may win the FA Cup!

20

ALL THINGS
BRIGHT AND BEAUTIFUL

Words: Cecil Frances Alexander (1818–95)
Music: William Henry Monk (1823–1889): *All Things Bright
and Beautiful*
Musical arrangement: Martin Shaw (1875–1958): *Royal Oak*
Musical arrangement for choirs: John Rutter (1945–)

*All things bright and beautiful,
All creatures great and small,
All things wise and wonderful,
The Lord God made them all.*

Each little flower that opens,
Each little bird that sings,
He made their glowing colours,
He made their tiny wings.

Chorus

The rich man in his castle,
The poor man at his gate,
He made them high or lowly,
And ordered their estate.

Chorus

The purple-headed mountains,
The river running by,
The sunset and the morning
That brightens up the sky;

Chorus

The cold wind in the winter,
The pleasant summer sun,
The ripe fruits in the garden,
He made them every one;

Chorus

[The tall trees in the greenwood,
The meadows where we play,
The rushes by the water
We gather every day.]

Chorus

He gave us eyes to see them,
And lips that we might tell
How great is God Almighty,
Who has made all things well.

Chorus

THIS SIMPLE HYMN for children celebrates the beauty of all things created by God, 'Maker of Heaven and Earth'. A Victorian bestseller, in the twentieth century it was cut and criticized, parodied, and even banned from English schools.

Its author Cecil Frances Alexander would be shocked and amazed at this reception. She was born in Dublin in 1818 and grew up in that city's Anglo-Irish community. She was the daughter of an English officer, Major John Humphreys and his wife Elizabeth (nee Reed). An army man, her father went on to manage the estates of the Earl of Wicklow. The 'redoubtable' Cecil Frances was also good-looking and was courted by two up and coming clergymen; she married one of them, Reverend William Alexander, in 1850. William rose through the Church of Ireland to become Archbishop of Armagh and Primate of All Ireland.

Cecil Frances developed an early love of, and talent for, religious poetry and was a prolific author of hymns and carols. Before her marriage she taught children in Sunday Schools and many of her hymns were written for these children. She published 'All Things Bright and Beautiful' in her book *Hymns for Little Children* in 1848 with a preface by a leading member of the Oxford Movement, John Keble – the Movement was an early influence on Cecil Frances. *Hymns for Little Children* became hugely popular and went to 100 editions – she gave its profits to a school for deaf mutes in Londonderry.

There are three main melodies for 'All Things Bright and Beautiful, as far as I'm concerned. The popular one was for a long time a lilting adaptation by Martin Shaw of a seventeenth-century Royalist tune *Royal Oak*, celebrating Charles II's 1660 Restoration and named after the oak tree where he's said to have hidden in 1651 on the long road to the English throne.

Shaw was a colourful musician and composer of songs, hymn tunes, orchestral works, and theatre music – he conducted for the actress Ellen Terry and toured with Isadora Duncan, whose orchestras he described as 'solid, stolid & squalid', a quote I adore! A great promoter equally of English music and of church music, he was, with his friend Ralph Vaughan Williams, music-editor of *Songs of Praise* (1925 and 1931) and *The Oxford Book of Carols* (1928).

I associate this hymn with two very different distinctive melodies – the tune of my youth by William Henry Monk and the melody of adulthood by John Rutter.

William Monk composed a fair number of popular hymn tunes, including one of the most famous from nineteenth-century England, *Eventide*, used for the hymn 'Abide With Me'. He also wrote music for church services and a number of anthems.

In 1874, Monk became a singing teacher at King's College, London. In 1876, he became a teacher at the National Training School for Music. In 1878, he started teaching at Bedford College. In addition, he was music director for almost four decades at St Matthias, Stoke Newington, London, and was the first musical editor for the historic hymnal *Hymns Ancient and Modern*, which sold 60 million copies.

Thomas Hardy wrote of Monk's editing for *Hymns Ancient and Modern*:

> Stripped of some of your vesture
> By Monk or another. Now you wore no frill,
> And at first you startled me. But I know you still,
> Though I missed the minim's waver
> And the dotted quaver.

More recently, the score for the hymn for choirs by John Rutter (1945–) has been on the repertoire of choirs and soloists worldwide.

It's quite unusual to find a hymn where different melodies for the same set of words are as popular as each other. I have grown up singing this hymn – firstly as a child in school assemblies singing the Monk melody, and then as an adult, performing the Rutter one. I have to admit to not having a clear favourite – all tunes serve the words just brilliantly. Although if I was pushed to proclaim a champion I would come down on the Rutter side because of the feeling of unadulterated joy and thanks conjured up by the pulsating lively melody.

Cecil Frances Alexander's words are quite simplistic and very direct – we are to celebrate the joyfulness of creation, and the composers mentioned, in my view, have managed to musically give this hymn a childlike innocence – a playfulness that further reinforces the message that God does indeed 'make all things well'.

Yet the words of this innocent hymn have fallen foul of modern sensibilities. Verse 6 for example:

> The tall trees in the greenwood,
> The meadows where we play,
> The rushes by the water
> We gather every day;

No longer appears in hymnbooks; its words are seen to be altogether too rural for the understanding of today's city children. Verse 3:

> The rich man in his castle,
> The poor man at his gate,
> God made them high or lowly,
> And ordered their estate.

Has bothered liberal society still more – and it's all about a comma. Set as above, Cecil Frances' words seem to be saying that God set out to order people into toffs and peasants, rich and poor, the lucky and unlucky. Insert a comma after 'them', thus: 'God made them, high or lowly', and Mrs Alexander's intention becomes rather less controversial.

Notwithstanding, this verse has vanished from today's hymnbooks following the lead of the ILEA (Inner London Education Authority), which in 1982 banned the hymn from use in its schools for its inegalitarian sentiments.

Parodies of 'All Things Bright and Beautiful' abound. Perhaps the most quotable being *Monty Python*'s 1980 (on *Monty Python's Contractual Obligation Album*) send-up:

> All things dull and ugly,
> All creatures short and squat,
> All things rude and nasty,
> The Lord God made the lot.
> Each little snake that poisons,
> Each little wasp that stings,
> He made their brutish venom,
> He made their horrid wings.

British comedy trio The Goodies' version on their 1978 *The Goodies Beastly Record* begins:

> All things bright and beautiful, all creatures great and
>   small
> The cuddly and the furry ones, I love to eat them all
>   (ohh, ohh, ohh)
> I am a carnivore, and I'm proud to say
> I eat meat for breakfast, tea and dinner every day
> I am a carnivore, I cannot deny it
> Moo cows, pigs and baa lambs are my staple diet . . .

But the hymn has also been a writer's inspiration. James Herriot chose his titles for his winning books about those Yorkshire vets from the hymn: his first, *All Creatures Great and Small*, subsequently became the title of the film and BBC television series. And for the books that followed, he used these lines: *All Things Bright and Beautiful*, *All Things Wise and Wonderful* and *The Lord God Made Them All*.

This hymn is a particular favourite of my daughter Emilia – and I must admit as a proud father that she gives a stunning performance of it in the shower. Who said hymns were only to be sung on a Sunday in church!

21

SHINE JESUS SHINE

Words and music: Graham Kendrick (1950–)

Lord, the light of Your love is shining,
In the midst of the darkness, shining,
Jesus, Light of the world, shine upon us,
Set us free by the truth You now bring us,
Shine on me, shine on me.

Shine, Jesus shine
Fill this land with the Father's glory
Blaze, spirit, blaze,
Set our hearts on fire
Flow, river flow
Flood the nations with grace and mercy
Send forth your word
Lord, and let there be light.

Lord, I come to Your awesome presence,
From the shadows into Your radiance
By the blood I may enter Your brightness,
Search me, try me, consume all my darkness,
Shine on me, shine on me.

Chorus

As we gaze on Your kingly brightness
So our faces display your likeness
Ever changing from glory to glory,
Mirrored here may our lives tell your story.
Shine on me, shine on me.

Shine, Jesus shine
Fill this land with the Father's glory
Blaze, spirit, blaze,
Set our hearts on fire
Flow, river flow
Flood the nations with grace and mercy
Send forth your word
Lord, and let there be light.

WRITTEN by singer/songwriter Graham Kendrick in 1987, 'Shine Jesus Shine' invokes the idea of a divine light that burns with a ferocity that can 'Set our hearts on fire'. It's a modern classic!

First and foremost, Graham Kendrick is a really, really lovely man and I've been fortunate to work with him on several occasions, on stage performing, also interviewing him for *Songs of Praise*. What's always come across is his passion for music and also of course his passion for his faith. Both come through in his songs, especially 'Shine Jesus Shine'.

Graham Kendrick was born in Blisworth, Northampton-shire in 1950. The son of a Baptist pastor, he has been doing his work as 'the father of modern worship music' since he started to write songs in the late 1960s, while touring the Christian coffee bar circuit as a member of the Christian beat group Whispers of Truth. He co-founded the 'March For Jesus' movement, which grew into an international prayer, praise and proclamation event, involving a total of around 55 million people over its years as a globally organized event. There are currently 67 Kendrick songs in the UK Christian Copyright Licensing International top 500. A remarkable achievment in anyone's book.

'Shine Jesus Shine' is his greatest hit so far. It is one of only two modern hymns in the *Songs of Praise* top ten, and it will forever be in the top ten. Children in the last twenty years have grown up with this hymn. It's instantly catchy, it has a great beat behind it; equally it can be sung without drums, it can be sung without electric guitar and it can be sung just with piano, as many schoolchildren do perform it up and down the country.

What's amazing is that this 'hit' was composed in an unremarkable way. Graham said, 'My longing for revival in the churches and spiritual awakening in the nation was growing', so he wrote the hymn's verses. But it was months later that the chorus would come to him. He said, 'I remember stand-ing in my music room with my guitar round my neck trying different approaches and then the line "Shine Jesus shine" came to mind and within half an hour I'd finished the chorus.' A world-changing hymn being finished in a short space of time – where have we heard that before?

I've performed this hymn quite a few times. I was very

lucky to witness Graham Kendrick performing it himself on one of the first Big Sing programmes we recorded for *Songs of Praise* from the Royal Albert Hall. (An event I will talk more about in this book.) It was an electrifying experience, six thousand Christians in one building and Graham Kendrick performing his most famous hymn with his band. Needless to say it went down incredibly well and I could see that this hymn was actually bringing people closer to God in the way that 'Abide With Me' does, in the way that 'Make Me a Channel of Your Peace' or 'Guide Me O Thou Great Redeemer' do. But in a different way too, this is a modern celebration of God, this is praising God wearing your contemporary heart very much on your sleeve.

I think Graham's had quite a bit of stick from traditionalists. He's all about being quite up front about your relationship with your God and the fact that you shouldn't hide away; the Church should be out there on the street, if you like, not hiding behind a closed door. This hymn supports his vision, it is a fantastic, uplifting performance hymn. You can't help but feel totally light of heart when you sing it.

Melody-wise it's very repetitive but this further rams home the message. A hymn should be a piece of music that everyone in the whole world can sing, probably on the second listening, and as far as 'Shine Jesus Shine' is concerned, I defy you not to be able to sing it after you've heard it once. It will be one of those tunes that stays in your head for the rest of the day. You're probably humming it now!

If I was a betting man, I'd say that out of all the modern worship songs that are now in existence, 'Shine Jesus Shine' will be up there with 'Dear Lord and Father of Mankind' and 'How Great Thou Art', being sung for the next millennia. It's a hymn that already in its short existence has come to mean so much to so many people. Having presented *Songs of Praise* for many years now, witnessing the joy in people's faces when they perform this, be it in Spain, or in the Albert Hall, or even actually the joy in Graham Kendrick's face when he played it in a little church in London with me between takes when I was interviewing him. His whole body and face transformed when he started strumming his guitar and the words 'Shine Jesus shine' came forth. It's what Graham Kendrick's about. He doesn't need to write an autobiography, all his passion and beliefs and the way he lives his life are encased in his greatest hit, 'Shine Jesus Shine'.

22

IMMORTAL, INVISIBLE, GOD ONLY WISE

Words: Walter Chalmers Smith (1824–1908)
Music: Welsh folk melody 'Can Mlynedd l'nawr', *St Denio*

Immortal, invisible, God only wise,
In light inaccessible hid from our eyes,
Most blessed, most glorious, the Ancient of Days,
Almighty, victorious, thy great name we praise.

Unresting, unhasting and silent as light,
Nor wanting, nor wasting, thou rulest in might;
Thy justice, like mountains, high soaring above
Thy clouds, which are fountains of goodness and love.

To all, life thou givest, to both great and small;
In all life thou livest, the true life of all;
We blossom and flourish as leaves on the tree,
And wither and perish – but naught changeth thee.

Great Father of glory, pure Father of light,
Thine angels adore thee, all veiling their sight;
All laud we would render; O help us to see
'Tis only the splendour of light hideth thee.

'I MMORTAL, Invisible, God Only Wise' is one of Queen Elizabeth's favourite hymns and it was chosen to be sung at the Chapel Royal, Windsor Castle to mark Her Majesty's 60th birthday on 21 April, 1986. It's all about celebration and praise, making it suitable as the first hymn sung at the beginning of a wedding service, which is in praise of God in whose presence everyone has assembled.

It also appears to be an essentially British hymn, sung at school assemblies the length and breadth of the land. Yet it was written by a Scot and is sung to a Welsh melody.

Its author Walter Chalmers Smith was a minister of the Free Church of Scotland. He was born in Aberdeen and was a grammar school boy and a student there, attending Marischal College at Aberdeen University. He was ordained on Christmas Day, 1850, pastor of the Chadwell Street Scottish Church in Islington, but the remainder of his ministry was back in Scotland, where he served in Milnathort near Kinross, in Edinburgh and Glasgow. He was made Moderator of the General Assembly of the Free Church of Scotland in its jubilee year, 1893.

Chalmers Smith was a liberal in the church and he was a respected poet. His collection *Olig Grange* was published in 1872. In the poem 'Olig Grange', Chalmers Smith writes, 'God giveth speech to all, song to the few.' He displayed the songster's art in the writing of hymns, the best-known of which, 'Immortal, Invisible', first appeared in his *Hymns of Christ and the Christian Life* in 1876.

The hymn is based on Timothy 1:17: 'Now unto the King eternal, immortal, invisible, the only wise God, be honour and glory for ever and ever.'

It is full of light; God is 'silent as light' and is hidden from us – paradoxically – in 'light inaccessible.' The last two lines of the first verse address: 'Most blessed, most glorious, the Ancient of Days / Almighty, victorious, Thy great name we praise.' This rich Aramaic title for God appears in many religions (and in Phillip Pullman's 'His Dark Materials' trilogy). These lines are based on the book of Daniel 7. Lines 13–14 read: 'I kept on beholding in the visions of the night, and, see there! With the clouds of the heavens someone like a son of man happened to be coming; and to the Ancient of Days he gained access, and they brought him up close even before that One.'

The resplendent 'Thy justice, like mountains, high soaring above / Thy clouds . . .' is from Psalm 36:6: 'Thy righteousness is like the great mountains.'

Chalmers Smith wrote a hymn of five verses. In 1884 the hymnologist William Garrett Horder (1841–1922) combined verses 4 and 5 for his *Congregational Hymns*. It's this four-verse version that we use today.

'Immortal, Invisible' is set to a Welsh folk song *St Denio* (also known as 'Joanna'). The Journal of the Welsh Folk Song Society proposes a ballad of about 1810, *Can Mlynedd I'nawr*, 'A Hundred Years from Now', as the likely source for *St Denio*. It appeared in 1839 as a hymn-tune in Wales' first hymn collection, *Caniadau y Cyssegr* edited by John Roberts who often used his bardic nom de plume 'Ieuan Gwylt' – Wild Ieuan.

Without John Roberts we wouldn't have the wealth of glorious Welsh hymns that we enjoy today. He was born at Tanrhiwfelen, a house just outside Aberystwyth in 1822, his father Evan was a precentor, his mother Elizabeth a fine vocalist. When he was still very young he wrote both poetry and music. He was most definitely a man ahead of his time. He led an amazing life – as well as writing poetry and composing music he was also a solicitor's clerk, a teacher, a periodical editor and publisher, a music festival founder and a minister. But his real life-work was collecting and selecting the best hymn tunes for use by the Welsh nation. He laboured for six years to produce in April 1859 *Llyfr Tonau Cynulleidfaol* (Congregational Hymn Singing) which single-handedly began a new exciting era in Welsh congregational singing. He continued throughout his life to inspire and encourage the amateur singer to learn these great Welsh tunes and use them as often as possible. He died in 1877 and was buried in Caeathro cemetery, near Caernarvon, where both my parents grew up.

This hymn first made an impact on me during my time at David Hughes Comprehensive School. It has an undulating tune with the first two musical phrases being quite similar and rather childish in quality. It's not until the third and fourth lines that you get the full impact of the beauty of the melody and one realizes how cleverly crafted this hymn actually is.

I've sung it many times since childhood and in many different situations – from being a pupil at school to my time as a chorister and then as a church goer – even on *Songs of Praise* during my time as a presenter on the programme, and I have to admit to not thoroughly enjoying the partnership of words and music for the first half of the verses but to really taking pleasure in the second half. My favourite lines to sing are: 'Thy justice, like mountains, high soaring above / Thy clouds, which are fountains of goodness and love.' I also enjoy: 'We blossom and flourish as leaves on the tree / And wither and perish – but naught changeth thee.'

Overall this is a good hymn that's easy to sing and the sense of celebration and praise does come through in abundance, in music and words, but unlike Her Majesty I would place it outside my top ten favourites.

23

LET ALL MORTAL FLESH KEEP SILENCE

Words: from the Liturgy of St James
Translation: Gerard Moultrie (1829–1885)
Music: 'Picardy' by Ralph Vaughan Williams (1872–1958)

Let all mortal flesh keep silence, and with fear and
   trembling stand;
Ponder nothing earthly-minded, for with blessing in
   his hand
Christ our God to earth descendeth, our full homage
   to demand.

King of kings, yet born of Mary, as of old on earth he
   stood,
Lord of lords, in human vesture – in the body and
   the blood –
He will give to all the faithful his own self for heav'nly
   food.

Rank on rank the host of heaven spreads its vanguard
   on the way,
As the Light of light descendeth from the realms of
   endless day,
That the powers of hell may vanish as the darkness
   clears away.

At his feet the six-winged seraph; cherubim with
   sleepless eye
Veil their faces to the Presence, as with ceaseless voice
   they cry –
Alleluia, alleluia, alleluia, Lord most high!

H ERE IS A HYMN of great age and mystery. Its first line commands us to be quiet, be fearful and give 'full homage' to this majestic God, who 'descendeth' with all the force of William Blake's supreme being surrounded by the seraphim and the cherubim singing multiple Alleluias at the tops of their voices!

Its ancient provenance is a ninth-century Greek version of the Liturgy of St James (associated with St James the Just) that can itself be traced back to the fifth century in the Eastern churches. The words of this hymn could have been written for the Offertory as the priest brings the Eucharistic gifts (bread and wine) to the altar for consecration and – in Catholic doctrine – celebrates the moment when Christ is escorted down by the heavenly host to be embodied in the Eucharist.

From its almost exotic beginnings, this hymn builds a bridge between the doctrines of Eastern Orthodoxy and the worship of Western Christians. Its foundations were laid with the 1869 translation of the Liturgy of St James by J. M. Neale (1818–1866) and R. F. Littledale (1829–1890) under the magnificent title: 'The liturgies of SS Mark, James, Clement, Chrysostom & Basil, and the Church of Malabar'. Neale was himself a gifted translator of ancient hymns from the Latin and Greek, considered to have a fine ear for melody in words, but musically he had 'not a note in his voice'.

Gerard Moultrie, who likely knew the Neale/Littledale prose version, versified the 'Prayer of the Cherubic Hymn', which appeared in *Lyra Eucharistica* in 1864. Born in Rugby and educated at Rugby School, his positions post-ordination included chaplain of Shrewsbury School and vicar of Southleigh, where he's buried. Gerard had a particular high-church spirituality, which is reflected in his work. He followed his father John Moultrie into hymnwriting and published his own *Hymns and Lyrics* in 1867. He did not work alone on this; his sister Mary Dunlop Moultrie (1837–1866) contributed a number of hymns to the collection, where they're distinguished by her initials. The brother and sister were close, and her early death had a long-term effect on Gerard Moultrie.

The tune for 'Let All Mortal Flesh Keep Silence' was published in the *English Hymnal* of 1906: Its music editor Ralph Vaughan Williams had been scouring the English countryside for English folk songs. They were vanishing fast and his project was to preserve and transcribe as many as he could find. He found this music beautiful and valued its roots in the unacknowledged working lives of ordinary people. He also began to use some of the melodies in his own work. The old folk tune, 'The Ploughboy's Dream', for instance, became the musical setting of 'O Little Town of Bethlehem'.

Vaughan Williams' source for 'Picardy', to which he put Moultrie's verses, comes from a French folk song 'La Ballade de Jesus Christ'. Vaughan Williams discovered the ballad in an 1860 collection of *Chansons Populaires des Provinces de France*.

He is of course one of England's great composers. His father, the Revd Arthur Vaughan Williams had been living at Down Ampney in Gloucestershire, where Ralph was born on

12 October 1872. Arthur died when his son was three years old; his mother Margaret Susan, great-granddaughter of the potter Josiah Wedgwood, took him to live with her at the Wedgwood family home at Leith Hill in the North Downs. Ralph went to school at Charterhouse and university at Trinity College, Cambridge. His musical education was at the Royal College of Music under Charles Villiers Stanford, where he made lasting friendships with, among many, Leopold Stokowski and Gustav Holst. He studied with Max Bruch in Berlin and in Paris with Maurice Ravel. He returned to the Royal College as Professor of Composition in 1921.

During his long and rich creative life he wrote, as The Ralph Vaughan Williams Society puts it, 'nine symphonies, five operas, film music, ballet and stage music, several song cycles, works for chorus and orchestra, and church music'. His music for hymns and carols includes what he calls an 'English traditional melody' for 'Firmly I Believe and Truly', as well as the lovely carol 'O Come, All Ye Faithful' and the joyful 'Sine Nomine' setting of 'For All the Saints'.

Many have noted how important it is to appreciate the spirit of 'Englishness' of Vaughan Williams' music. He died aged eighty-five on 26 August 1958. Fifty years later, Stephen Pollard observed in *The Times* newspaper that 'Vaughan Williams was the last composer to speak directly to a wide audience . . . there is an indefinable Englishness about almost everything he wrote.'

This is a hymn that I first came to perform when I was at Bangor Cathedral. and I remember thinking as a twelve year old what an honour it was to be singing such music. It's not at all a normal hymn. Talking about Vaughan Williams, Sir John Barbirolli had it that, 'He loved life, he loved work and his interest in all music was unquenchable and insatiable'. With this hymn, he had the brilliance to marry an ancient Greek version of a still older chant and set it to the melody of a French folk ballad – and it has that French feel to it.

My favourite verse is the third one: 'Rank on rank the host of heaven spreads its vanguard on the way'. A van and a guard? As a ten year old, I had to ask Dr Andrew Goodwin, who was my choirmaster at Bangor Cathedral, to put me right on the meaning of this word. Then 'As the light of light descendeth from the realms of endless day / That the powers of hell may vanish as the darkness clears away' – such great writing.

These days if you were to mention 'Let All Mortal Flesh Keep Silence' to me, I'd think of a young saxophonist called Christian Forshaw, who has recorded this piece of music. He set up a group called Sanctuary with a fine singer, Grace Davidson and they'd recorded an ethereal version of the hymn, with saxophone and voice and keyboard. A dear lady called Julie Nicholson heard this recording on Classic FM. She was a Vicar in Bristol at the time, but she was finding it impossible to celebrate communion with her parishioners since her daughter Jenny had been killed at Edgware Road in the bombings of 7 July 2005. She felt unable to forgive her daughter's killers, so she stood down as a priest from her parish of St Aidan at St George in Bristol. Sitting in her car, listening to Christian Forshaw's version of 'Let All Mortal Flesh Keep Silence', she found comfort in the piece of music and contacted Christian to tell him so. Their friendship grew and Christian wrote a piece of music especially for Julie's daughter. So powerful can a hymn be that someone who is unable to forgive, can find comfort and strength in it. I was fortunate to interview both Julie and Christian on my BBC

Radio 2 program *Good Morning Sunday* and we also played this piece of music. The response from listeners was phenomenal. It was an incredibly emotional moment and one that will remain with me always. This hymn always resonated to me but now, since getting to know Christian and Julie it means a great deal more to me. I see this music as blessed.

24

THINE BE THE GLORY

Words: Edmond L. Budry (1854–1932)
Translation: Richard B. Hoyle (1875–1939)
Music: George Frideric Handel (1685–1759)

Thine be the glory, risen, conquering Son,
Endless is the victory thou o'er death hast won;
Angels in bright raiment rolled the stone away,
Kept the folded grave-clothes where thy body lay.

Thine be the glory, risen, conquering Son,
Endless is the victory thou o'er death hast won.

Lo, Jesus meets us, risen from the tomb;
Lovingly he greets us, scatters fear and gloom;
Let the Church with gladness hymns of triumph sing,
For her Lord now liveth, death hath lost its sting.

Chorus

No more we doubt Thee, glorious Prince of Life;
Life is nought without thee: aid us in our strife;
Make us more than conquerors through thy deathless love;
Bring us safe through Jordan to thy home above.

Chorus

THIS HYMN sings exultantly of Christ's resurrection. Its three stanzas are inspired by the gospel accounts of the resurrection, and notably St Paul in 1 Corinthians 15, who declares triumphantly, 'death has lost its sting'. Edmond Budry, who wrote the original words in French and set them to a tune by Handel, was a Swiss pastor. He composed the hymn when he was in mourning for his first wife Marie, who had just died. He seems to have wanted to offer himself and extend to all believers the reassurance that death is not the final word, and that due to Christ's resurrection he would see his beloved wife again.

The hymn does indeed celebrate Christ the conqueror of death, and in the last verse it entreats us to be more than conquerors ourselves, and to be brought to everlasting life though Christ's love 'bring us safe through Jordan to thy home above'. For Christians this is such an important message to get across – life after death – and I sincerely hope that this is indeed the case.

Edmond Budry was born in Vevey, Switzerland, studied theology in Lausanne and later returned to work as pastor of the Free Evangelical Church in Vevey for a full thirty-five years. He retired in 1923.

His words were translated into English by a remarkably multi-lingual Baptist pastor called Richard B. Hoyle. He was born in 1875, in Cloughfold, England. He attended Regent's Park College in London from 1895 to 1900. He then served as a Baptist minister in several churches in England for twenty-six years. After that, he worked with the YMCA and for some time edited their publication called *The Red Triangle*.

Hoyle translated about thirty French hymns into English. He also translated hymns from twelve other languages, all of which he read fluently. In 1934 he went to the United States, where he taught at Western Theological Seminary in Philadelphia for two years. On returning to England, he became the pastor of the Baptist church in Kingston-upon-Thames.

The tune of 'Thine Be the Glory' preceded the words. Budry had been listening to an Advent hymn sung to a tune by George Frideric Handel for the chorus 'See the Conquering Hero Comes' in *Judas Maccabaeus* (1746). He wrote the words to fit the tune and it first appeared in print in English in the *Cantate Domino* (1924).

Judas Maccabaeus was, after the *Messiah*, Handel's most popular oratorio. He composed it when he was sixty-one and had been living in England for twenty-five years. It celebrates a rather different kind of conquering hero, William, Duke of Cumberland and his victory over Charles Edward Stuart the Pretender at the battle of Culloden on 16th April 1746. It was first performed in London at the Covent Garden Theatre the following year. But so popular is this tune that it has been used for many other purposes as well as this hymn. It would for instance also be familiar to Prom-goers, as one of the movements in Sir Henry Wood's *Fantasia on British Sea Songs* (1905), often played at the Proms, and to nineteenth-century rail enthusiasts as the tune played by brass bands at the opening of new railway lines and stations. More recently it has been played as the theme tune for the BBC coverage of the 2006 football World Cup.

This hymn has such a majestic, powerful feel to it – the words are very passionate and muscular – 'glory, conquering, victory, triumph, glorious'. It's also a very positive hymn to sing. This is most definitely one for the congregation as a whole to enjoy. Preferably with huge organ and brass accompaniment! I don't think it would work as well as a solo.

25

NEARER, MY GOD, TO THEE

Words: Sarah Flower Adams (1805–48)
Music: J. B. Dykes (1823–76): *Horbury*
Arthur Sullivan (1842–1900): *Propior Deo*
Lowell Mason (1792–1872): *Bethany*

Nearer, my God, to thee,
Nearer to thee!
E'en though it be a cross
That raiseth me,
Still all my song shall be,
Nearer, my God, to thee,
Nearer to thee!

Though, like the wanderer,
The sun gone down,
Darkness be over me,
My rest a stone,
Yet in my dreams I'd be
Nearer, my God, to thee,
Nearer to thee!

There let the way appear
Steps unto heaven;
All that thou sendest me
In mercy given;
Angels to beckon me
Nearer, my God, to thee,
Nearer to thee!

Then, with my waking thoughts
Bright with thy praise,
Out of my stony griefs
Bethel I'll raise;
So by my woes to be
Nearer, my God, to thee,
Nearer to thee!

Or if on joyful wing
Cleaving the sky,
Sun, moon, and stars forgot,
Upwards I fly,
Still all my song shall be,
Nearer, my God, to thee,
Nearer to thee!

THE STONE transformed from pillow to pillar, the dream of steps unto heaven, and beckoning angels – all clues to the Biblical source of this well-known hymn.

'Nearer, My God, to Thee' springs from the story, in Genesis 28. 10–22, of Jacob and his covenant with God: 'Now Jacob went out from Beersheba and went toward Haran. So he came to a certain place and stayed there all night, because the sun had set. And he took one of the stones of the place and put it at his head and he lay down in that place to sleep. Then he dreamed, and behold a ladder set up on the earth, and the top of it reached to heaven: and behold the angels of God ascending and descending on it.'

In the hymn it is the wandering singer who yearns to climb the angel-populated ladder, then to dispense with it altogether and fly, 'Cleaving the sky' in order to be 'Nearer my God to thee, Nearer to thee!'

Sarah Flower Adams wrote these verses. She was the younger daughter of Benjamin and Eliza Flower. Her father was a radical journalist and her elder sister Eliza a musician and composer. To begin with, Sarah worked as an actress and she did apparently get to play Lady Macbeth, but her health was poor (she died of tuberculosis aged 43), so she turned to the gentler profession of writing. Her dramatic poem 'Vivia Perpetua' was published in 1841, also the year that 'Nearer, My God, to Thee' appeared in print.

The hymn might never have got into print, but Sarah and Eliza attended the Unitarian South Place Chapel in Finsbury and it was common practice at the time for chapels to have their own hymnbooks. The minister, William Johnson Fox, was putting together a book of *Hymns and Anthems* designed for singing in his chapel. He invited Sarah to include a number of her hymns in his collection and 'Nearer, My God, to Thee' was one of the thirteen she contributed. Its musical setting was provided by Eliza. From this small beginning, the hymn has had a long, successful life.

A Unitarian, Sarah had reservations about the religious orthodoxy of her times. Her scepticism grew through her friendship with the young poet Robert Browning; it also got her hymn into trouble with higher church Christianity. She met Browning through Eliza and talked with him about his religious dilemmas: 'It was in answering Robert Browning', she wrote, 'that my mind refused to bring forward argument, turned recreant, and sided with the enemy.'

William Walsham How (1823–97) was not exactly the enemy, but he disliked the Unitarian colour of Sarah Flower's verses and set out to write a 'paraphrase' expressing 'more definitely Christian faith, and better adapted for congregational worship'. His version begins, 'Nearer to Thee My God'. He was the author of the hymn 'For All Thy Saints', a good man, known for his work with the poor, but in this instance he should have known better. Despite his efforts, it's the original words that have lasted and proved popular with worshippers.

Since Eliza Flower's setting for this hymn, there have been a few more: best known is *Horbury* by John Bacchus Dykes, after the Lancashire village of that name. It was published in the 1861 first edition of *Hymns Ancient and Modern*. I've talked about Dykes elsewhere in this book, in relation to 'Holy! Holy! Holy!' for example, and 'Lead Kindly Light'. In the US the hymn is sung to *Bethany* by the founder of the Boston Academy of Music, Lowell Mason. Arthur Sullivan's tune *Propior Deo* first published in *The Hymnary*, Novello, 1872, is also a respected version. Sullivan wrote hymn tunes in abundance, at least seventy-two of them, mostly in the years before his opera career with W. S. Gilbert started, including 'Onward Christian Soldiers', which I've also chosen for this book, and 'It Came Upon the Midnight Clear'. Writing hymns and popular songs helped him to earn his living. Sullivan was a boy soloist for the choir of the Chapel Royal, in London, and his first published work was the song 'O Israel', written when he was thirteen years old.

Survivors of the RMS *Titanic* have a story to tell about 'Nearer, My God, to Thee'. It's a tragic story. Wallace Henry Hartley (1878–1912), who played the violin, was employed to lead the eight-member band that entertained passengers on the great White Star ship's maiden voyage. When the *Titanic* started to sink, Hartley and his band played music to calm the passengers who were being loaded into the lifeboats. None of the band members survived. People who witnessed the sinking from the boats have insisted that the band carried on to the bitter end and that 'Nearer, My God, to Thee' was the last piece they played. Hartley's was body number 224 to be recovered; he was buried in his hometown of Colne in Lancashire. 40,000 people lined the route of his funeral procession.

The opening notes of Sullivan's *Propior Deo* are written on Hartley's memorial, though whether he and the band played this or the *Horbury* version on the *Titanic* is not entirely clear. He was British and would have known the *Horbury* tune, but he was also the son of a Methodist choirmaster, who had often used Sullivan's *Propior Deo* setting for the hymn. 'Nearer, My God, to Thee' is played by Hartley's band in all three British features made about the disaster: Negulesco's *Titanic* (1943), *A Night to Remember* (Roy Ward Baker, 1958), where it is played to *Horbury*, and James Cameron chose, most probably in error, to use *Bethany* for his *Titanic* of 1997.

Another *Titanic*-inspired film featuring the hymn has a different slant. On a barge on a lake the punk rock trio Green Day is giving a concert. The lake is Springfield Lake, the film *The Simpsons Movie* (2007), and the audience is the entire population of that toxic town. When Green Day stop rocking the *Simpsons* theme tune and start to talk about the environment, the crowd gets nasty, the barge begins to sink, eaten up by the toxicity of the waters, and the doomed band strike up 'Nearer, My God, to Thee' on violins. Just before their total immersion, bassist Mike Dirnt quotes Hartley's final words from Cameron's *Titanic*: 'Gentleman, it's been an honour playing with you tonight.'

A massive owning-up session here, that for the first thirty-eight years of my live, I've never sung a note – or a word – this magnificent hymn. I'm not sure why, but if there's one hymn on my 'to do' list in the recording studio, it's this one. The chances are that the album that comes out to accompany this book will have on it my first performance and recording of 'Nearer, My God, to Thee'. It's anthemic in its grandeur.

I've heard it performed many times and one of the most moving performances was by Daniel O'Donnell in the Royal Albert Hall. The collective 'oohs' and 'aahs' from the audience that evening proved to me what a direct and dramatic effect this piece has on us – this effect can maybe explain why it was played while the *Titanic* went down.

That night, when Daniel O'Donnell sang it, we were recording the Big Sing for *Songs of Praise*. It's a glorious evening filled with hymn music. We basically record two very important programmes in one night – one, which celebrates some of our greatest hymns and the other programme is a Christmas special. I have been involved in the Big Sing for many years and it's one of the highlights in my calendar year. Me, and the other six thousand people who manage to cram into the Royal Albert Hall! Tickets for this event sell out in a matter of minutes, such is the demand. Who said that hymns don't sell! I realized then that you don't have to do much to put across a strong and well-written hymn. Daniel stood there in the middle of the stage under the spotlight. He didn't move, he didn't do much with his voice, he simply sang the song and the message came through loud and clear. It was a moving experience for me backstage and for the thousands who were there listening to him.

26

THERE IS A GREEN HILL FAR AWAY

Words: Cecil Frances Alexander (1818–95)
Music: William Horsley (1774–1858): *Horsley*

There is a green hill far away,
Without a city wall,
Where the dear Lord was crucified
Who died to save us all.

We may not know, we cannot tell,
What pains he had to bear;
But we believe it was for us
He hung and suffered there.

He died that we might be forgiven,
He died to make us good,
That we might go at last to heaven
Saved by his precious blood.

There was no other good enough
To pay the price of sin;
He only could unlock the gate
Of heaven, and let us in.

O dearly, dearly has he loved,
And we must love him too,
And trust in his redeeming blood,
And try his works to do.

IF EVER YOU WANTED a hymn with a direct message and a direct story, then this is it. It tells you everything you need to know in the first two lines, 'There is a green hill far away / Without a city wall / Where the dear Lord was crucified / Who died to save us all'. There you go, end of message. It's written in a very childlike way, but it gets to the heart of the story immediately.

Cecil Frances Alexander wrote it for her godson. It's a familiar story, he'd been complaining about learning the catechism, how difficult and dull it could be. Cecil Frances understood children and was involved in their religious education. She set about writing a group of hymns designed to help him and other pupils learn the truths of the Creed in a simpler and more interesting way. 'There is a Green Hill Far Away' is one of these. It explains simply and candidly the frightening words in the Apostles' Creed: 'Suffered under Pontius Pilate, was crucified, dead and buried'. She published 'There is a Green Hill Far Away' alongside 'All Things Bright and Beautiful' and more in her bestselling *Hymns for Little Children* of 1848. What a talent this lady had!

Though crystal clear in its meaning, the first line of the hymn can be puzzling. Where is this distant hill? Why would it need a city wall in the first place? Modern hymnbooks have made the simple change from 'without' to 'outside' the city wall. Also, Cecil Frances lived for a long time in Londonderry. There was apparently a grass-covered mound just outside the town, which moved her to imagine a hill in the Holy Land beyond Jerusalem's gates where Christ came to be crucified. It is a hymn written with a depth of emotion and meaning suggesting both that Christ loved us dearly and that he paid dearly for this love.

The tune for this hymn was written by William Horsley, founder member of the Philharmonic Society and a figure who occupied the heart of the musical establishment in London during the late 1790s. He became organist at the Asylum for Female Orphans and assistant to John Wall Callcott, whose eldest daughter Elizabeth Hutchins Callcott (1809–72) he married. He succeeded Callcott in 1802 and held the post at the asylum for fifty-two years. He was also organist of the Charterhouse in London, a teacher, and in his later years he was a friend of Mendelssohn. His tune for 'There is a Green Hill Far Away', which he named *Horsley*, is his best known hymn composition.

It's a hymn that I first sang in primary school in Welsh and in English and I remember that all of us used to look forward to Easter, not because we were treated in any different way, it was just that we were allowed to sing this moving hymn. It's interesting that William Horsley, an upstanding member of the musical establishment, also wrote glees, or part songs. They were drinking songs and songs that expressed idyllic or fraternal sentiments and could occasionally be remarkably risqué. They were sung in gentleman's clubs in Britain, primarily in London. It's intriguing that he wrote successful glees and was well known in that world and also contributed to the composition of this stunning melody.

The tune is a joy to sing. In childhood I remember it was probably one of the first hymns where we were told to change the dynamic in our voices. As a child you can sing 'There is a Green Hill' in a full voice and I recollect the headmaster at the time at Llandegfan Primary School, a musician himself, suggesting that for the second verse we could change the intensity and use half the volume. He explained that the 'feeling' inside us would be so different. So my fellow pupils and I sang 'O dearly, dearly has he loved / And we must love him too' in a more intimate fashion and instantly realized that there were shades to be had in hymn singing and it wasn't always just full pelt. I'll always remember that moment in assembly on a rainy morning in my village primary school.

This gorgeous hymn was also included on a CD I made with the BBC Welsh Chorus called *Voices from the Holy land*. We went out to Israel to film three TV programmes for BBC1, which proved to be extremely popular when aired. A CD was released which shot into the pop charts. There was something so special watching the marvelous chorus sing this hymn in the actual place it was describing. It was a very spiritual experience.

Many adults shy away from singing this hymn because they see it as immature and there are certain cathedral choirs that aren't very happy tackling it for the same reason, but it's for that same reason I think it's a very strong composition. Its strength lies in its uncomplicated quality. It tells an unsurpassable story and the melody to go with the words is unusual because it doesn't take you to the most obvious of places. You can tell that the composer wasn't just a church organist, he also wrote symphonies for full orchestra and wrote part songs for unaccompanied voices. This is an incredibly well crafted melody and a real joy to sing. If you don't acknowledge it because it's childish, you're missing a real treat with this hymn.

27

I VOW TO THEE MY COUNTRY

Words: Cecil Spring-Rice (1859–1918)
Music: Gustav Holst (1874–1934): *Thaxted*

I vow to thee, my country, all earthly things above,
Entire and whole and perfect, the service of my love:
The love that asks no question, the love that stands the
    test,
That lays upon the altar the dearest and the best;
The love that never falters, the love that pays the price,
The love that makes undaunted the final sacrifice.

And there's another country, I've heard of long ago,
Most dear to them that love her, most great to them
    that know;
We may not count her armies, we may not see her king,
Her fortress is a faithful heart, her pride is suffering;
And soul by soul and silently her shining bounds
    increase
And her ways are ways of gentleness and all her paths
    are peace.

TODAY, this elegant hymn can be seen to evoke a distant England of patriotic public school values, of service and sacrifice. In H. E. Bates's words: 'the past is another country, they do things differently there.' Yet this hymn also quotes from Proverbs 3:17 claiming a different other country, a heavenly kingdom, whose 'ways are ways of gentleness and all her paths are peace'.

'I Vow to Thee My Country' was written by a quietly heroic man. Cecil Spring-Rice was a career diplomat. He was sent out by the Foreign Office to far-flung cities including Tehran and Petrograd and was finally despatched to Washington in 1913 with the brief to persuade the US to abandon its neutral stance and enter the war. There he remained until 1918. 'He steered his course with unfailing judgement and unwearied forbearance,' wrote Arthur Balfour, 'at a time when a single false step might have had the most serious consequences for the cause which he represented.'

The words of 'I Vow to Thee My Country' came into being in two stages, and represent perhaps a tidal change in Spring-Rice's beliefs. The first version was written as the poem 'Urbs Dei' (The Two Fatherlands) during his time in Stockholm between 1908 and 1913. Later, in January 1918, recalled from Washington and on the eve of his departure for England, he re-worked his first stanza that had perhaps glorified too much the kind of patriotism promoted at the time. 'The greatest object of all,' he now wrote to a friend, 'at the most terrific cost and the most tremendous sacrifice – will, I hope, at last be permanently established, Peace.'

Stopping in Ottawa on the way home, a month after he'd completed his re-write of 'Urbs Dei', Spring-Rice died suddenly. A contemporary summed up the nature of his heroism: 'He gave his life for his country as surely as though he had been slain in battle.'

The hymn reached a wide audience when it was printed by Percy Dearmer in *Songs of Praise* in 1925. It now had its setting, to a piece extracted from Gustav Holst's 'Jupiter' in his orchestral suite *The Planets*. Holst named this tune *Thaxted*, after the Essex village where he lived with his wife Isobel and daughter Imogen, who followed her father into music as composer, conductor and for two decades artistic director of the Aldeburgh Festival.

Holst was born in Cheltenham – into music – his grandfather played and taught the harp, his father Adolph von Holst was an organist, pianist and choirmaster, his mother Clara a singer. Gustav (who played the trombone) was educated at Cheltenham Grammar School for Boys and at the Royal College of Music, where he met his lifelong friend Ralph Vaughan Williams. The influences on his music were rich and varied: English folk songs, the poetry of Whitman and Thomas Hardy were inspirations, so was Hindu mysticism and spirituality.

Holst was a keen rambler, traveller, and astrologer. Astrology was his 'pet vice', but it also informed his best known work. Holst started working on *The Planets* suite at Thaxted. The first, electric, recording of the suite was in 1926, with Holst himself conducting the London Symphony Orchestra. It became his most popular work and made Holst a famous man. He hated the publicity this brought. He would hand eager fans who asked for his autograph a card, which read 'I do not hand out my autograph'. He died in London and his ashes were placed in Chichester Cathedral.

I live in South West London and on the stretch of road called 'The Terrace' there's a lovely property with a blue plaque on the wall stating that Holst lived there between 1908 and 1913. It has over the years become a bit of a Jones' household habit to launch into a line of 'I Vow To Thee' as we pass the house. I pray that the current owners don't hear!

Holst was a socialist of the school of Shaw and William Morris and 'I Vow to Thee My Country' has been debated and quoted by modern politicians – of all sides. In 1988, Margaret Thatcher addressed the General Assembly of the Church of Scotland. In her 'Sermon on the Mound', she spoke of her conviction that each individual will be saved: '[I Vow to Thee My Country] speaks of "another country I heard of long ago" whose King can't be seen and whose armies can't be counted, but "soul by soul and silently her shining bounds increase",' she said.

Mrs Thatcher did not have the last word, however. Singer-songwriter Billy Bragg and Martin Linton, the current Labour MP for Battersea, later composed a new version of the hymn, which begins:

> We vow to build a country
> Where all can live in health,
> Where no child need live in poverty,
> Where we will share our wealth;
> Where we fill the true potential
> Of each and every one
> And we achieve more together
> Than we achieve alone.

Hymns written when the past was another country tend to draw later debate about interpretation. 'I Vow to Thee My Country' attracted this kind of controversy a few times. In 2004, for example, the Right Reverend Stephen Lowe, Anglican Bishop of Hulme took the lines: 'I vow to thee, my country, all earthly things above / Entire and whole and perfect, the service of my love' and found them heretical. 'It's saying my country right or wrong', he argued, it puts an individual's love for country above their relationship with God. Debate this time was about the meaning of 'country' in the hymn, and whether 'entire and whole and perfect' refers to country or to 'the service of my love'.

This is another hymn that is popular with current recording artists. It was recorded by Welsh soprano Charlotte Church on her debut album *Voice of an Angel* (1988), when she was twelve years old, by Welsh mezzo-soprano Katherine Jenkins on her third album *Living a Dream* in 2005, and in the same year by G4 on their album *G4 and Friends*, which reached number six in the UK charts. It's even been sung by the English cricket team.

I have been singing hymns for over thirty years and I'm amazed that I have never performed this piece. I honestly don't know why and I am surely going to rectify the situation soon. I've sung it at home recently and it creates in you an immense feeling of power – it's definitely a hymn to get the blood pumping round your veins. It's a hugely patriotic hymn in the same vein as 'Guide me O Thou Great Redeemer'.

'I Vow to Thee My Country' is regularly used on Remembrance Day through the Commonwealth nations. It was also chosen by Diana Spencer to be sung at her wedding to Prince Charles in July 1981. It had, she said, 'always been a favourite since schooldays'. On 9 September 1997, it was again sung for Diana at her funeral by the congregation and the millions worldwide who followed the service on television and radio. Every time I hear this hymn it reminds me of her beaming smile and heartfelt warmth.

28

WE PLOUGH THE FIELDS AND SCATTER

Words: Matthias Claudius (1740–1815)
Translation: Jane Montgomery Campbell (1817–78)
Music: Johann Abraham Peter Schulz (1747–1800)

We plough the fields, and scatter
The good seed on the land,
But it is fed and watered
By God's almighty hand:
He sends the snow in winter,
The warmth to swell the grain,
The breezes, and the sunshine,
And soft, refreshing rain.

All good gifts around us
Are sent from heaven above;
Then thank the Lord, O thank the Lord,
For all his love.

He only is the maker
Of all things near and far;
He paints the wayside flower,
He lights the evening star;
The winds and waves obey him,
By him the birds are fed;
Much more to us, his children,
He gives our daily bread.

Chorus

We thank thee then, O Father,
For all things bright and good,
The seed-time and the harvest,
Our life, our health, our food:
Accept the gifts we offer
For all thy love imparts,
And, what thou most desirest,
Our humble, thankful hearts.

Chorus

'WE PLOUGH the Fields and Scatter' gives thanks to God for the fruits of the earth and the abundance of nature especially at harvest time. With its clear and positive theme and cheerful melody it has a deep popular appeal, especially for children.

This is another hymn that transports me back to primary school at Llandegfan, the village I grew up in on the isle of Anglesey in North Wales. I have vivid memories of sitting cross-legged on the wooden floor with all my fellow students, about a hundred and fifty of us, singing along to 'We Plough the Fields and Scatter'. It takes me back to the smells of lunch being prepared in the kitchen behind the shutters to the right of where I sat, and to the headmaster with guitar in hand. I can even hear the individual teachers' voices coming through the massed din as we wholeheartedly sang this hymn.

Harvest was always a very happy time at Llandegfan primary school. We'd spend time preparing our boxes of fruit and vegetables and then present them in assembly and then at the local parish church. I have very fond memories of learning this hymn for the very first time. It seems incredible to me that even at the age of six or seven, I realized that we had a lot to thank God for: 'He sends the snow in winter, the warmth to swell the grain / The breezes and the sunshine / And soft, refreshing rain'. I remember chuckling at that last line when I was a child – I never thought of the rain as refreshing, rather that I wouldn't be able to go out and play football. And let me tell you, it rained a lot in North Wales. And I loved to play football.

Singing this harvest hymn, it feels as if it must have come direct from the British countryside but it actually has German origins. It was based on a peasant's song and its author, Matthias Claudius, is said to have heard local farmers singing it one evening in Northern Germany where he was working as an editor of the local newspaper and Commissioner of Agriculture.

If ever we should thank the lord for editors, then this hymn is proof of that. Matthias Claudius originally wrote seventeen verses, but when it was first published in 1800 in a collection of melodies for schools, the editors obviously took pity on the children of this country and it was cut down to six. Thankfully, most of the time these days we have three verses to sing. This version was translated into English by Jane Montgomery Campbell. She is otherwise known for compiling two children's hymnbooks. Hers was not a literal translation, but it preserves the spirit of the original.

The son of a clergyman, Matthias Claudius seemed destined to become one himself but took to journalism instead and became one of Germany's most popular writers and poets. In 1771 he became editor of the *Wandsbeck Messenger*, a small German newspaper produced four times a week but with a circulation of only about four hundred. Claudius soon had Germany's most renowned writers contributing, including the great Goethe, and made it a notable paper of its day. He also published a large number of his own prose essays and poems in his paper, written under the pseudonym 'Asmus', and in pure and simple German which appealed to the popular taste. In 1817, Franz Schubert set to music as a song Claudius's poem *Death and the Maiden,* and in 1824 this song in turn he re-wrote as the string quartet of the same name.

The patron of the *Wandsbeck Messenger* Duke Heinrich von Schimmelmann was a rich trader who owed much of his wealth to the slave trade. Notwithstanding, Claudius used the paper to speak out against slavery. In 1773 he published in it an article, 'Der Schwarze in der Zuckerplantage' ('The Black Man in the Sugarcane Plantation') that is now regarded as the first statement against slavery in German literature.

The tune for 'We Plough the Fields and Scatter' was composed by the German musician and composer, Johann Abraham Peter Schulz. His musical interests ranged widely; he wrote stage music and folk songs, operas and cantatas.

In this age of agribusiness and pesticides, 'We Plough the Fields and Scatter' conjures up another age when things were simpler and purer. Updated versions of the hymn have been written to reflect modern farming methods – 'We plough the fields with tractors, with drills we sow the land' is one. It was John Betjeman, acutely aware of the changes going on around him, who recorded on the BBC in 1969 the most memorable of these:

> We spray the fields and scatter
> The poison on the ground.
> So that no wicked wild flowers
> Upon our farms be found.
> We like whatever helps us
> To line our purse with pence;
> The twenty-four-hour broiler house
> And neat electric fence.
>
> All concrete sheds around us
> And Jaguars in the yard,
> The telly lounge and deep freeze
> Are ours from working hard.
>
> We fire the fields for harvest,
> The hedges swell the flame,
> The oak trees and the cottage,
> From which our fathers came.
> We give no compensation,
> The earth is ours today,
> And if we lose on arable,
> The bungalows will pay.

Good as the Betjeman is, I can't really see it being sung at the local church in the near future! Here's another classic that has made it into my list of favourites because of its childlike quality and simplicity. It also celebrates one of my most loved times of year.

29

IN CHRIST ALONE

Words and music: Keith Getty (1974–)
and Stuart Townend (1963–)

In Christ alone my hope is found;
He is my light, my strength, my song;
This cornerstone, this solid ground,
Firm through the fiercest drought and storm.
What heights of love, what depths of peace,
When fears are stilled, when strivings cease!
My comforter, my all in all—
Here in the love of Christ I stand.

In Christ alone, Who took on flesh,
Fullness of God in helpless babe!
This gift of love and righteousness,
Scorned by the ones He came to save.
Till on that cross as Jesus died,
The wrath of God was satisfied;
For ev'ry sin on Him was laid—
Here in the death of Christ I live.

There in the ground His body lay,
Light of the world by darkness slain;
Then bursting forth in glorious day,
Up from the grave He rose again!

And as He stands in victory,
Sin's curse has lost its grip on me;
For I am His and He is mine—
Bought with the precious blood of Christ.

No guilt in life, no fear in death—
This is the pow'r of Christ in me;
From life's first cry to final breath,
Jesus commands my destiny.
No pow'r of hell, no scheme of man,
Can ever pluck me from His hand;
Till He returns or calls me home—
Here in the pow'r of Christ I'll stand.

T HE MANY remarkable and prolific hymn writers of the
past who are celebrated in this book have still too few
modern successors. Keith Getty is one person who has
mastered the art of modern hymnody. Stuart Townend is
another. Together they wrote 'In Christ Alone'. Its power for
me is in the first two lines – and they state so clearly what this
hymn is about: 'In Christ alone my hope is found/He is my
light, my strength, my song'. The lyrics that Stuart Townend
created really do say it all. They fit perfectly with the simple,
beautiful melody. Getty and Townend have created a song
that allows the singer to sing it from the heart and mean every
single word. I've sung it as part of a congregation and I love
the fact in the first few lines Christ is seen as being a song, as

my faith is centred around music. As far as I'm concerned, like Graham Kendrick's 'Shine Jesus Shine', 'In Christ Alone' is another classic contemporary Christian hymn.

'In Christ Alone' also tells a big story in little form: of Christ's life from 'helpless babe' to the Resurrection, through a folk melody that has a simple and strong connection with people living their lives in the world. It may be this that has helped to make 'In Christ Alone' among the most popular Christian songs ever sung and it's a great testament to Keith Getty and Stuart Townend that their hymn has remained in the *Songs of Praise* top twenty, where there are usually only a handful of modern hymns. This one is always highest in the league. It's also in the CCLI (Christian Copyright Licensing International) Top Songs list in the UK, Australia, Canada and the US.

'In Christ Alone' is a striking expression of this quest for a lasting relevance. It is the first song Keith co-wrote with Stuart and it was released on the Kingsway album *New Irish Hymns*, with vocalists Maire Brennan, Margaret Becker and Joanne Hogg. It has since been recorded over a hundred times, including arrangements by the Newsboys and Natalie Grant. Many hymns have followed, crossing musical genres and bridging generations, including 'Beneath the Cross of Jesus', 'Speak, Oh Lord' and 'Don't Let Me Lose My Wonder'.

Keith Getty is a man on a mission: with his wife, composer and artist Kristyn Getty, he has set out to write and perform really contemporary hymns because he believes that this is an art that must be revived for our generation and beyond. 'There are two reasons we write modern hymns,' Keith Getty says. 'First, it's to help teach the faith. What we sing affects

how we think, how we feel and ultimately how we live . . .
The second reason is to try and create a more timeless
musical style that every generation can sing, a style that relates
to the past and the future.'

Julian Keith Getty was born in Lisburn, Northern Ireland.
He had a Christian upbringing and his musical education
started aged eleven, when he took up classical guitar. He went
on to learn the flute. During a summer masterclass with Sir
James Galway, it was not so much Getty's mastery of the flute
that appealed to the famed flautist as his piano arrangements,
and this encounter set him on the road to a successful career
in the music industry. His faith and his intention to communicate through music the basic truths of Christianity to the
widest world congregation were confirmed while he was
studying music at university in Durham.

Getty is a skilled orchestrator; he has arranged lots of
music for media, from McDonald's TV commercials to
recordings for Sir Cliff Richard, from compositions for the
African Children's Choir, to the orchestration of Ennio
Morricone's music on disc. He has also composed for such
gospel artists as Natalie Grant. In 1994, he started the New
Irish Choir and Orchestra.

Stuart Townend is the son of a West Yorkshire Church of
England vicar and the youngest of four children. Like Getty,
he started his musical education early; he has been playing the
piano since he was seven and as a teenager he taught himself
to play the guitar. It's said that the particular power of his
songwriting lies in its lyricism and its theological depth. As
Townend himself says, 'If you can express in songs the profound truth of the gospel in a poetic yet accessible way, they
really can have an impact in people's lives.' These strengths can

be felt in 'In Christ Alone'. He has continued to work with Keith and Kristyn on other liturgically based songs, including 'The Power of the Cross' and 'Behold the Lamb'.

I've been lucky to interview Stuart Townend many times and he comes across as a very modest man with an honest faith. The fact that he tries to live his life through Christ in a positive way comes through in him when you meet him and also in his writing. He's a man that wears his Christian heart on his sleeve. Hard to imagine that the co-writer of 'In Christ Alone' always wears a baseball cap — even on *Songs of Praise*! And gets fewer complaints than I do when I don't wear a tie!

These new pioneers have together produced a twenty-first century hymn that will appeal down the generations, just as those of John Newton, the Wesleys, or Cecil Frances Alexander have endured to the present.

30

ON A HILL FAR AWAY STOOD AN OLD RUGGED CROSS (THE OLD RUGGED CROSS)

Words and music: George Bennard (1873–1958)

On a hill far away stood an old rugged cross,
The emblem of suffering and shame;
And I love that old cross where the dearest and best
For a world of lost sinners was slain.

So I'll cherish the old rugged cross
Till my trophies at last I lay down;
I will cling to the old rugged cross
And exchange it some day for a crown.

O, the old rugged cross, so despised by the world,
Has a wondrous attraction for me;
For the dear Lamb of God left his glory above
To bear it to dark Calvary.

Chorus

In the old rugged cross, stained with blood so divine,
A wondrous beauty I see;
For 'twas on that old cross Jesus suffered and died
To pardon and sanctify me.

Chorus

To the old rugged cross I will ever be true,
Its shame and reproach gladly bear;
Then he'll call me some day to my home far away,
Where his glory forever I'll share.

Chorus

THE AUTHOR of this beloved hymn for Good Friday had a vision: 'I saw the Christ and the cross inseparable', George Bennard wrote in his memoirs. The weathered 'old rugged cross' he returns to repeatedly is more than a religious symbol, it stands at the heart of the gospel, of Christ's suffering – and the Christian experience.

Born in Ohio, Bennard grew up in a poor family, with five brothers and sisters. He was of Scottish descent; his father George Russell Bennard is described as a taverner, who when his tavern burned down, became a coal miner. He died in an accident in the mine aged forty-nine and George, aged sixteen, followed him to work in the coalfield to support his mother Margaret and siblings. At this time he started to attend Salvation Army meetings, becoming a minister when he was twenty-four years old.

George Bennard became a travelling Methodist evangelist. He was known as a strong speaker, a sharp dresser and a good man. He settled in Albion, Michigan, where in the early 1900s it is thought he opened his own hymn publishing company and wrote most of his many hymns and gospel songs, such as 'Speak, My Lord' and 'Oh, Make Me Clean'. He seems to have been one of those people we describe as hiding their light under a bushel, or perhaps he was just a modest man. He apparently once said, somewhat ruefully, 'I've been introduced as the author of "The Old Gray Mare", "The Old Oaken Bucket", and even "Rock of Ages"; I've even been introduced as George Bennard Shaw, the English philosopher!'

'The Old Rugged Cross' soon became a popular gospel song in the revivalist tradition, and it was first sung at a revivalist meeting to Bennard's own musical setting (the famed gospel-song composer Charles H. Gabriel may have helped him with his harmonies). It came to the attention of Ashley 'Billy' Sunday, one of the most renowned evangelist preachers around in the cities of the USA during the early 1900s. This former major league baseball player was also an athletic preacher, known for his conversational style and fast and furious delivery. He took up the song on his campaigns through the cities of America and brought 'The Old Rugged Cross' to a wide audience; in 1921 it was recorded and radio helped it to reach further still, notably as performed during the 1940s on his radio show by 'King of the Cowboys' Roy Rogers.

Meanwhile, Bennard continued his evangelistic ministries. He died at the age of 85, near Reed City, Michigan. Nearby stands a tall cross with the words '"The Old Rugged Cross" – Home of George Bennard, composer of this beloved hymn.'

'The Old Rugged Cross' is popular with many of the most important recording artists of the twentieth century. It's been recorded by a host of them, including Al Green, the Queen of Gospel Mahalia Jackson, by Patsy Cline and Loretta Lynn, by Tennessee Ernie Ford, Jim Reeves, Johnny Cash and June Carter, Chet Atkins, and of course Elvis. He only sang great hymns like 'How Great Thou Art', 'Amazing Grace' and of course, this one. In Wales as a child, I heard it one Sunday morning being played on my parents' radio and I actually got myself out of bed – a rare occurrence when I wasn't singing at the cathedral – to find out who the voice was, and it was Elvis performing this amazing piece of music.

On television, Dennis Potter used the hymn in several of his dramas, notably *Pennies from Heaven* (1978). Much later, in an episode of *Doctor Who*, gridlocked in New York on a nightmare motorway going nowhere, the trapped motorists sadly sang 'The Old Rugged Cross', before they were liberated by David Tennant's Time Lord.

During the twentieth century, 'The Old Rugged Cross' established itself as a UK favourite. It was one of the most requested hymns by viewers of *Praise Be!*, which Thora Hird presented for BBC television for seventeen years from 1977. Since then though it has started to be seen as an old fashioned hymn. Maybe the answer to its popularity decline lies in the fact that 'The Old Rugged Cross' is a popular song in popular form with verse pattern and three-four time signature and this puts it in danger of being quite sentimental.

And for George Bennard, it was a hymn about the Christian's experience rather than the adoration of God. I'm a great fan of such personal hymns, because you can put your own stamp on them. That so many twentieth-century greats recorded it suggests that they understood this quality in it. It seems that no one really has since. Don't ask me why!

You can describe 'The Old Rugged Cross' as either a song or a hymn. To me it's both. It's hymn-like in quality but I'd always seen it as a solo piece. At a recent *Songs of Praise* recording I saw it listed on the song sheet as a congregation hymn and it was with some trepidation that I stood in amongst the crowd anticipating the start of 'The Old Rugged Cross'. I didn't see how it could work sung in this way, but I was wrong. The minute the chorus kicks in: 'So I'll cherish the old rugged cross / Till my trophies at last I lay down; / I will cling to the old rugged cross / And exchange it some day for a crown', it works brilliantly. It's another of those 'big' hymns that seems to unite a congregation.

This is definitely a hymn I'd love to record in the future. The biggest dilemma I envisage having will be, do I go the straight congregation-style route or do I go for the Elvis!

31

HOLY! HOLY! HOLY!
LORD GOD ALMIGHTY

Words: Reginald Heber (1783–1826)
Music: John Bacchus Dykes (1823–76)

Holy! Holy! Holy! Lord God Almighty!
Early in the morning our song shall rise to thee;
Holy, Holy, Holy! merciful and mighty!
God in three Persons, blessed Trinity!

Holy, Holy, Holy! all the saints adore thee,
Casting down their golden crowns around the glassy sea;
Cherubim and Seraphim falling down before thee,
Which wert, and art, and evermore shalt be.

Holy, Holy, Holy! though the darkness hide thee,
Though the eye of sinful man thy glory may not see,
Only thou art holy, there is none beside thee
Perfect in power, in love, and purity.

Holy, Holy, Holy! Lord God Almighty!
All thy works shall praise thy name in earth and sky and
sea;
Holy, Holy, Holy! merciful and mighty!
God in three Persons, blessed Trinity!

Alfred Lord Tennyson considered this hymn to be the finest in the English Language; on 11 October 1892 it was sung at his funeral in Westminster Abbey. It is also the best possible hymn to be sung on Trinity Sunday – addressing directly and simply, 'God in three Persons'.

'Holy! Holy! Holy!' thrives on its combination of images from the Old Testament and the New. The promise that 'Early in the morning our song shall rise to Thee', is from Psalm 63:1: 'Early I will seek thee', which is also the Epistle for Trinity Sunday in the Book of Common Prayer. Inspiration for the wonderful assembly of saints 'casting down their golden crowns around the glassy sea' is the 'sea of glass like unto crystal' of Revelation, Chapter 4:6.

Reginald Heber, who wrote 'Holy! Holy! Holy!', was one of the first great migration of clergymen dispatched by Britain in the early nineteenth century to live dangerously, spreading the gospel through the world. He was also an innovator in the history of hymnology.

Heber was born in Malpas in Cheshire, where his father was rector. He was a gentleman and a precocious scholar – it's claimed that he'd read and understood the Bible in full by age five! He went to Brasenose College, Oxford where he was a student and poet of distinction, was made fellow of All Souls in 1804, and having taken Holy Orders in 1807, he became rector of Hodnet in Shropshire.

Heber rose through the Church of England and in 1823 he was sent out to India as Bishop of Calcutta. His diocese was large, he travelled throughout the East converting the heathen, establishing schools, consecrating churches.

He'd expressed his sense of the missionary's task in the hymn 'From Greenland's Icy Mountains', written while at Hodnet:

> . . . From India's coral strand,
> Where Afric's sunny fountains
> Roll down their golden sand;
> From many an ancient river,
> From many a palmy plain,
> The call us to deliver
> Their land from error's chain.

Thus far with glorious imagery, this verse however follows:

> What though the spicy breezes
> Blow soft o'er Ceylon's isle;
> Though every prospect pleases,
> And only man is vile?
> In vain with lavish kindness
> The gifts of God are strown;
> The heathen in his blindness
> Bows down to wood and stone.

Such sentiments were common among this first generation of missionaries and the hymn was hugely popular in its time. However, it is no doubt that this imperialist thinking has lost this hymn to modern hymnals.

The backbreaking work killed Reginald Heber: after three years in India, at the age of forty-three, he died in his bath from a cerebral haemorrhage.

Heber's hymns are his memorial. He wrote most of them, including 'Holy! Holy! Holy!', as well as 'Brightest and Best of the Sons of the Morning' and 'By Cool Siloam's Shady Rill', while at Hodnet. But they were not published until after his death. He had, he said, 'some High Church scruples against using them in public'. 'Holy! Holy! Holy!' appeared first in *A*

Selection of Psalms and Hymns for the Parish Church of Banbury in 1826.

He was strict, priggish even, in his approach to hymn writing. 'I avoid all fulsome, indecorous or erotic language', he wrote, 'to HIM whom no unclean lips dare approach'. But he was also an innovator: Betjeman places him as 'the first specifically liturgical hymn-writer of the Church of England', because he wrote a hymn for every Sunday and most solemn and feast days in the Church of England calendar. Including of course this one for Trinity Sunday.

John Bacchus Dykes wrote the resplendent tune of 'Holy! Holy! Holy!', which was first published in the original, 1861 edition of *Hymns Ancient and Modern*. He named it *Nicaea*, fittingly after the Council of Nicaea, called by Constantine I in 325 to defend the doctrine of the Trinity from the heretical claims of Arius and his followers. *Nicaea* is considered the finest melody of this most prolific – he composed three hundred hymn tunes – and popular of composers. He was a Yorkshireman, born in Hull. Like Reginald Heber, he showed early talent and was already assistant church organist aged ten. He spent most of his life in the North East, including his time as canon, then precentor of Durham Cathedral and as vicar of St Oswald's, Durham and marked his affection for the region by naming many of his tunes after northern saints and places.

Dykes' music for the hymn has a processional beat, which was not lost on soldiers in the First World War. They adapted its words to express the wet weariness of

> Marching, marching marching,
> Always bloody well marching,

and:

> Raining, raining, raining,
> Always bloody well raining.
> Raining in the morning,
> And raining in the night.
>
> Grousing, grousing, grousing
> Always bloody well grousing
> Grousing at the rations,
> And grousing at the pay.
>
> Marching, marching, marching
> Always bloody well marching,
> When the war is over,
> We'll damn well march no more.

'Holy! Holy! Holy!' instantly transports me back to my early days in Bangor Cathedral. This was a hymn we choristers loved to sing – it was never a case of losing one's head in the hymn book because we knew every verse started the same way so vocal levels were always on maximum! If as a boy I ever doubted that being a chorister was worthwhile this was the hymn that reinforced to me the fact that I loved to sing – and that as choristers we could touch people's hearts and souls.

The hymn is so deliberate in its construction – re-emphasizing the doctrine of the Trinity and the spiritual force one feels when launching into the final verse is awe-inspiring.

32

WHAT A FRIEND WE HAVE IN JESUS

Words: Joseph Medicott Scriven (1819–86)
Music: Charles Converse (1834–1918): *Converse*
Music: William Penfro Rowlands (1860–1937): *Blaenwern*

What a friend we have in Jesus,
All our sins and griefs to bear!
What a privilege to carry
Everything to God in prayer!
O, what peace we often forfeit,
O, what needless pain we bear,
All because we do not carry
Everything to God in prayer!

Have we trials and temptations?
Is there trouble anywhere?
We should never be discouraged:
Take it to the Lord in prayer.
Can we find a friend so faithful,
Who will all our sorrows share?
Jesus knows our every weakness:
Take it to the Lord in prayer.

Are we weak and heavy-laden,
Cumbered with a load of care?
Precious Savior, still our refuge:
Take it to the Lord in prayer.
Do thy friends despise, forsake thee?
Take it to the Lord in prayer;
In His arms He'll take and shield thee,
Thou wilt find a solace there.

Blessed Saviour, Thou hast promised Thou wilt all our
    burdens bear
May we ever, Lord, be bringing all to Thee in earnest
    prayer.
Soon in glory bright unclouded there will be no need
    for prayer
Rapture, praise and endless worship will be our sweet
    portion there.

THIS LOVELY HYMN is another which is childlike in quality and has the unadorned message about how proud we are to have that moment of prayer with God. I sang it at primary school and I think that sometimes there's nothing wrong with harking back to those simpler times. I remember what it felt like to sing this hymn as a small boy and I wish that my life now were sometimes as straightforward and safe. 'What a Friend We Have in Jesus' is what I would call a comforting hymn. The fact that this hymn is uncomplicated and easy to understand, makes it in my humble opinion a great hymn.

It's fitting that the writer of a hymn that speaks of God's consolation in times of hardship and distress, had a life of tragedy and suffering himself. Born and bred in Banbridge, Co Down, Joseph Medicott Scriven studied at Trinity College, Dublin. He had decided on pursuing a military career, which was prevented by the ill-health that continued through his life. He fell in love with a Banbridge girl, but the night before his wedding, his fiancée was trying to cross a bridge over the River Bann when she was thrown from her horse and drowned in full view of Scriven, who was waiting for her on the opposite bank. Grief-stricken, he decided to emigrate to Canada, where he settled at Rice Lake and then at Port Hope, Ontario. He fell in love again and became engaged to be married a second time only to be bereaved before the wedding ceremony once more because his fiancée died after a short spell of pneumonia. Devout and philanthropic, Scriven dedicated himself to working for the poor and destitute while earning his living as a tutor. A practical Christian, he was apparently known as the man who sawed wood for poor widows and sick people who were unable to pay.

Sadly 'What a Friend We Have in Jesus' was not published during his lifetime. It is said that a neighbour, sitting with him during his final illness, found the manuscript and liked it immediately. Apparently Scriven told him he wrote it to comfort his mother who was having her own sorrows in Ireland and that he did not intend anyone else to see it. When asked how he came to write such a beautiful hymn Scriven replied simply: 'The Lord and I did it between us.'

One reason the hymn has become so popular must be that the source of the words is the writer's own experience of repeated, seemingly inexplicable suffering. His response was not to succumb to despair or depression, but rather to find comfort and trust in the care of the Lord through appealing to

Him in prayer. This must resonate with many people who sing this hymn today who have troubles and suffering of their own.

William Penfro Rowlands' tune *Blaenwern*, composed for 'Love Divine', is also in the list of settings for 'What a Friend We Have in Jesus'. But even though I'm a fan of my Welsh melodies, I have to say that for me the music by Charles Converse fits it best. He was born in Warren, Massachusetts and studied music in Germany, where he became friends with Franz Liszt. He also composed symphonies, oratorios and gospel songs.

Soldiers in the First World War made 'What a Friend We Have in Jesus' their own. This version was used in the 1969 film *Oh What a Lovely War* and is not so much a parody, more a cry from the heart:

> When this lousy war is over,
> No more soldiering for me,
> When I get my civvy clothes on,
> Oh, how happy I shall be.
> No more church parades on Sunday,
> No more putting in for leave,
> I shall kiss the sergeant-major,
> How I'll miss him, how he'll grieve.

Much more recently, 'What A Friend We Have in Jesus' has become a favourite of the Japanese and has been translated many times.

I've seen and heard this hymn performed in a variety of ways. You can have the all-singing, all-dancing, up-tempo version, which almost needs an 'altogether now!' after the first few lines: 'What a friend we have in Jesus / All our sins and griefs to bear! / What a privilege to carry / Everything to God in prayer!

The other way of doing it is a lot more 'Gospel' in style and I think the melody has been composed in a way that really does allow you to do it your way, it can even be sung as a ballad because the words of this hymn are so strong and simple that they can stand the test of slowing down the melody. I love the idea that in this hymn Jesus is seen as your mate as opposed to a king-like reverential figure. In this hymn He's someone who's always there to listen to our prayers until as it says in the last verse we won't need prayer as we'll be in Heaven.

> Blessed Saviour, Thou hast promised Thou wilt all our
>   burdens bear
> May we ever, Lord, be bringing all to Thee in earnest
>   prayer.
> Soon in glory bright unclouded there will be no need
>   for prayer
> Rapture, praise and endless worship will be our sweet
>   portion there

And I take great comfort in this hymn for that reason.

33

JESU, LOVER OF MY SOUL

Words: Charles Wesley (1707–88)
Music: John Bacchus. Dykes (1823–76): *Hollingside*
Music: Joseph Parry (1841–1903): *Aberystwyth*

Jesu, lover of my soul,
Let me to thy bosom fly,
While the nearer waters roll,
While the tempest still is high;
Hide me, O my Saviour hide,
Till the storm of life is past;
Safe into the haven guide,
O receive my soul at last!

Other refuge have I none,
Hangs my helpless soul on thee;
Leave, ah, leave me not alone,
Still support and comfort me.
All my trust on thee is stayed,
All my help from thee I bring;
Cover my defenceless head
With the shadow of thy wing.

Thou, O Christ, art all I want;
More than all in thee I find;
Raise the fallen, cheer the faint,
Heal the sick, and lead the blind.
Just and holy is thy name,
I am all unrighteousness;
False and full of sin I am,
Thou art full of truth and grace.

Plenteous grace with thee is found,
Grace to cover all my sin;
Let the healing streams abound,
Thou of life the fountain art;
Freely let me take of thee;
Spring thou up within my heart,
Rise to all eternity.

MRS MARY HOOVER of Bellefonte in Pennsylvania relates this dramatic event in the lives of Charles Wesley and her grandmother Jane Lowrie Moore. Jane was the wife of a farmer and they lived in the parish of Killyleagh, County Down. Their house was a part of the Island Barn Farm there. Charles Wesley was preaching in the fields nearby, when he was set upon by men who opposed his beliefs. Wesley ran for it and found refuge in the Moores' house. Jane hid him in the milkhouse down the garden. The noisy mob arrived and demanded Wesley's whereabouts, but she quietened them down and gave them refreshments. While they ate and drank, she went to the milkhouse and released Mr Wesley through its rear window, to hide under a hedge. A little brook ran past his hiding-place. It was there, it's said, 'with the cries of his pursuers all about him', that he wrote 'Jesu, Lover of My Soul'.* You really couldn't make it up could you?

How to encompass the gifts Charles Wesley has given to both hymnology and the sheer ordinary pleasure of singing hymns? 'Jesu, Lover of My Soul' is a good place to begin.

It is a fiercely personal hymn that somehow calls intimately to Jesus the Saviour – its drama is of human proportions. It rolls like its stormy 'nearer' waters, and flows with its abundant 'healing streams'. Fittingly the psalms, those song-poems of the Old Testament, provide the hymn with a wealth of imagery, helping Wesley to bring the protection of the Saviour from the 'storm of life' up close, with images of safety: 'the haven' (Psalm 107); 'shadow of thy wing' (Psalm 91).

It was published in 1739 in *Hymns and Sacred Poems*, a year after Charles Wesley's conversion (the hymn he wrote to mark that occasion was 'Where shall my won'dring soul begin?'). He was the third surviving son of Samuel and Susanna Wesley's eighteen children and he grew up in Epworth, Lincolnshire. He was educated at Westminster, then followed his elder brother John to Christ Church, Oxford, where Charles formed the Holy Club, whose members were nick-named 'Methodists'. He thus laid down the foundations of Methodism, which was to him and to John, who became its leader, a revival movement remaining within the Church of England.

In 1735, the brothers followed the social reformer James Edward Oglethorpe to his new colony of Georgia, but they returned the next year and set out on their mission through Britain, preaching and frequently confronting mob opposition

* An apocryphal story this may be, but . . .

such as Charles experienced in Killyleagh: 'His preaching at its best was thunder and lightning', said one of the early Methodists. When the itinerant life became too much for him, Charles settled with his wife Sarah in Bristol, then in 1771, in Chesterfield Street, Marylebone. He was a hymnwriter to the end. On his deathbed in 1788, he dictated to Sarah:

> In age and feebleness extreme,
> Who shall a helpless worm redeem?
> Jesus, my only hope Thou art,
> Strength of my failing flesh and heart,
> O, could I catch a smile from Thee
> And drop into eternity.

'Jesu, Lover of My Soul' has been set to two fine tunes. John Bacchus Dykes' *Hollingside* was published in the first edition of *Hymns Ancient and Modern* in 1861. He named it after his cottage in Northumberland. His sister recalled sitting on the veranda listening to him composing the tune on the piano, 'in the deepening twilight of a calm Sunday evening'.

The *Aberystwyth* setting is the more popular. This tune was composed by Joseph Parry. He was born in Merthyr Tydfil, but when he was twelve, the family emigrated to Danville in Pennsylvania. While he worked there in the furnaces as an ironmaster, his real love was music. On his return to Britain, he studied music and in 1873, became Professor of Music at the University of Wales. He was a member of the Masonic lodge in Aberystwyth, was organist there, and wrote his first opera *Blodwen* – its first performance took place at the Temperance Hall in 1878 and it was a tremendous success. The author and playwright Jack Jones (1884–1970), a Merthyr lad like Parry, wrote the novel *Off to Philadelphia in the Morning*, based on Parry's life. This was dramatized by the BBC in 1978.

'Jesu, Lover of My Soul' has attracted criticism and praise both theological and personal throughout its history. William Gladstone did not like it, his reasons: 'It has no unity, no cohesion, no procession and no special force'. The great nineteenth-century Congregationalist preacher Henry Ward Beecher did like it, proclaiming: 'It will go on singing until the trump brings forth the angel band; and then I think it will mount up on some lip to the very presence of God.'

It has also attracted many tales; perhaps the most moving of these concerns the soldier fighting the American Civil War, who was poised to shoot another from the opposing side when he heard him singing, 'Cover my defenceless head / With the shadow of thy wing', and laid down his rifle.

Through my work on *Songs of Praise* I am very fortunate to have the opportunity to perform these hymns all over the world. Sometimes singing live, on other occasions miming to my own voice. I have two stories to share with you. My own tale of 'Jesu, Lover of My Soul' begins in the National Showcaves Centre for Wales – I kid you not – where I filmed this hymn for *Songs of Praise*. We went into the Dan yr Ogof caves, which are in South Wales, and then some time later emerged with 'Jesu, Lover of My Soul' filmed for *Songs of Praise*. It's an amazing place; there are lots of stalagtites and stalagmites in their commonest form, but the rare feature are the helictites, which grow out sideways. In the Cathedral Show Cave you can walk behind two forty-foot high waterfalls and experience its extreme natural beauty and there's a part of the cave that they call the dome of St Paul's. So it was like filming in the truest form of a cathedral, this being God's ultimate creation underground. I remember handing my voice recording of 'Jesu, Lover of My Soul' to the hardened 'I've seen it all' soundman from London and he turned round and said, 'Blimey, it's a dirge isn't it!' I didn't know what to say! I tried to explain to him that it's an incredibly powerful hymn with a typical Welsh melody, Welsh through and through, by Joseph Parry. I went to rehearse with my tail between my legs.

So these amazing vast caverns were our home for what felt like an age. We went in in the morning and we came out at midnight and our clothes were soaking wet from the atmosphere within these caves. It was an incredible experience for soundman, cameraman, director and myself. I was convinced I would never experience anything like that again. Well, that was until I found myself miming to the hymn on a vast snowy mountain top in South America. Huge birds soaring and not a cloud in the sky. We had the whole peak to ourselves – I was literally on top of the world, in heaven!

For me what makes 'Jesu, Lover of My Soul' is the music by Joseph Parry. There are many other melodies written for these words by Charles Wesley. Don't get me wrong, the words are good but not in my view, his finest. The great hymnwriter Charles Wesley wrote thousands and thousands of hymns, but what Joseph Parry has done is to give this one a really Welsh feel, it's all about singing from the heart and indeed it has been sung with passion in churches and chapels across Wales for well over a century.

It's a hymn of two halves musically. The first two lines are quite simple in their construction and the melody does more or less the same thing. Then the intensity starts to build up: 'Hide me, O my Saviour hide / Till the storm of life is past', followed by the highlight of the first verse: 'Safe into the haven guide', then you can take it right down in dynamic again to 'O receive my soul at last!'. And it's the same with the final verse; it takes you to the ultimate musical place: 'Plenteous grace with thee is found / Grace to cover all my sin / Let the healing streams abound' and again the second part of the melody kicks in and you can feel the pulse beginning to race: 'Thou of life the fountain art / Freely let me take of thee / Spring thou up within my heart / Rise to all eternity'. It's incredibly emotive and performing it in the caves and in South America were out-of-this-world experiences. I've never performed it on any other stage. Doubtless I will in the future, but at this point in my career it was those experiences that made 'Jesu, Lover of My Soul' for me.

Going back to my dear friend the London soundman, Eric, who mentioned that this hymn was a dirge. Well, I decided to go away and do some research and discovered that a dirge is a sombre song expressing mourning or grief but actually the word 'dirge' is derived from the Latin 'dirige domine deus meus in conspectu tuo viam meam', the first words in the first antiphon in the matins, which actually mean 'direct my way in your sight Oh Lord my God'. So Eric had it spot on because that is exactly what this hymn is about, directing one's life to God. So I shouldn't have taken umbrage with him saying that it was a dirge because, in a way, it is.

34

WHEN I SURVEY
THE WONDROUS CROSS

Words: Isaac Watts (1674–1748)
Music adapted: Edward Miller (1735–1807): *Rockingham*

When I survey the wondrous cross,
On which the Prince of Glory died,
My richest gain I count but loss,
And pour contempt on all my pride.

Forbid it, Lord that I should boast
Save in the death of Christ my God;
All the vain things that charm me most,
I sacrifice them to His blood.

See from His head, His hands, His feet,
Sorrow and love flow mingled down;
Did e're such love and sorrow meet,
Or thorns compose so rich a crown?

His dying crimson, like a robe,
Spreads o'er his body on the tree;
Then am I dead to all the globe,
And all the globe is dead to me.

Were the whole realm of nature mine,
That were an offering far too small,
Love so amazing, so divine,
Demands my soul, my life, my all.

I FIRST SANG this hymn at the Cathedral in Bangor many years ago. Before we began to sing, how it came to be written was always put into context. I thought then and still think that the story of this hymn is almost as great as the hymn itself. It was written by Isaac Watts, who has been described as 'the father of English hymnody'. What a title! As a teenager young Watts complained to his father about the monotonous way Christians in England sang the Old Testament psalms. So his dad, who was a deacon, turned round and said, all right young man, you give us something better. And he did. I think he's got a passion for poetry, rhyming and at the same time his hymn is real, that's the great thing about it. He was unattractive and sickly as a child, but also a prodigy, studying Latin when he was four, mastering Greek when he was nine, French at eleven, Hebrew at thirteen – he obviously didn't have any distractions such as television!

At fifteen, Watts' hymn-writing career began. What I like about all Issac Watts' hymns, and this one in particular, is that it's got all the theology in there, but also its verses have got plainness and power so that you understand where he's coming from and what he's trying to talk about: 'I would neither indulge in any bold metaphors,' he wrote, 'nor admit of hard words'.

Watts was also responsible for 'Oh God Our Help in Ages Past', another fine hymn, 'There is a Land of Pure Delight', and 'Come, Let Us Join Our Cheerful Songs' – the list goes on, to over six hundred. 'When I Survey the Wondrous Cross' is popularly thought to be his best hymn; some have gone so far as to call it the best hymn in the English language. The great thing about it is that it's only sixteen lines, particularly when you consider that a hymn like 'Battle Hymn of the Republic' features over a hundred. And these are sixteen perfect lines. It paints a wonderful picture of Christ's death on the cross, coupled with the love that we offer in return. I remember an interviewee I was working with on *Songs of Praise* once said that this is almost as if the words and music were written at the foot of the cross itself.

My favourite verse is definitely: 'See from His head, His hands, His feet / Sorrow and love flow mingled down / Did e'r such love and sorrow meet / Or thorns compose so rich a crown?' And also: 'Love so amazing, so divine / demands my soul, my life, my all'. There's complete commitment there in those two lines. It's as if the soul and the life aren't enough – I give my all.

The tricky moment for the singer and the congregation is on the word 'sorrow', because you don't sing it as it's written down. The tendency, because of the way the music moves, is to emphasize the second syllable of 'sorrow'. When the congregation sing the hymn, during the recording of *Songs of Praise,* the phone goes a few times. It'll be the music supervisor, trying to get us to sing this line just that little bit better. The fact that I'm nit-picking about one little syllable tells you how great a hymn this really is.

35

THE LORD'S MY SHEPHERD, I'LL NOT WANT

Words: Psalm 23
Music: Jessie Seymour Irvine (1836–87): *Crimond*
Music: James Leith Macbeth Bain (1840–1925): *Brother James' Air*
Music: Howard Goodhall (1958–)

The Lord's my shepherd, I'll not want
He makes me down to lie
In pastures green; he leadeth me
The quiet waters by.

My soul he doth restore again,
And me to walk doth make
Within the paths of righteousness,
Ev'n for his own name's sake.

Yea, though I walk in death's dark vale,
Yet will I fear no ill;
For thou art with me, and thy rod
And staff me comfort still.

My table thou hast furnished
In presence of my foes;
My head thou dost with oil anoint,
And my cup overflows.

Goodness and mercy all my life
Shall surely follow me,
And in God's house for evermore
My dwelling-place shall be.

I T'S REMARKABLE that a committee, drawing on various
sources, has created this beautiful hymn that seeps into
your bloodstream. The committee members could not really
go far wrong because the verses of 'The Lord's My Shepherd'
are rooted in a great Psalm. Psalm 23 was originally used in
Jewish worship, then sung in Latin plainsong, but the story of
this hymn in its current form begins in 1650 when the first
English version was published in the *Scottish Psalter*. This was a
collection of 'metrical psalms', paraphrased into the vernacu-
lar poetry of church hymns and it was written and compiled by
the Westminster Assembly (who also produced *The Book of
Common Prayer*). Today, even though the words are taken almost
directly from the Book of Psalms and are very old fashioned in
their construction, this hymn still means a lot to the more
modern congregation or audience – it still does hit the mark.

'The Lord's My Shepherd' takes the singer on a journey
from this world to the next – and to eternal life. Christ as
the Good Shepherd has so much resonance with the approach
of death, offering the qualities of protection and strength
needed at this time. His rod and staff is portrayed across
Christian art as the shepherd's crook, which can keep off the
wolves and provide comfort. Shepherds themselves appear
with their flocks from time to time through the Old and New
Testaments and of course they were there in Bethlehem for
the birth of Christ.

The Westminster Assembly's version of Psalm 23 wasn't known very much outside the Church of Scotland until nearly three hundred years later in the late 1920s, when the Glasgow Orpheus Choir sung it to the tune *Crimond*. The choir under its founder and conductor Sir Hugh Robertson, brought music to millions of people with its recordings and broadcasts on the early wireless. The version of the hymn they performed was printed in the 1929 *Scottish Psalter*.

There is some controversy over who wrote the tune *Crimond*. Most attribute it to Jessie Seymour Irvine, a 'talented amateur' in the writing of metrical psalm melodies. She was born in Scotland in 1836, her father was pastor in the village of Crimond in Aberdeenshire, and she is said to have written the tune when she was a teenager as an exercise for an organists' class she attended. Others suggest that 'Crimond' was written by an Aberdeen tobacconist, David Grant, but most agree today that he had a role only in its arrangement and appearance in print, and not in its composition. There have been settings for the hymn since by Irving Berlin, Leonard Bernstein, John Rutter and a truly heavenly version by my very good friend Howard Goodall. You may know this version as the theme music used for the brilliant BBC comedy series The Vicar of Dibley. My name was used in vain in the comedy once – I'm described as being testicularly challenged! Charming!

This is a hymn that I've been singing since I was a very young child. The words have remained the same but I've probably sung it in all its various settings. I've even performed Leonard Bernstein's 'Chichester Psalms' with Leonard Bernstein, one of the highlights of my life, and there's a setting of the hymn in the original Hebrew included in Leonard

Bernstein's 'Chichester Psalms' of 1965. I think the John Rutter version is beautiful; Howard Goodall's 'The Lord's My Shepherd' is a lilting masterpiece which has very quickly become a firm favourite with the choirboys. But I suppose the *Crimond* tune written by Jessie Seymour Irvine is the one that's most stuck in my mind. It's actually quite a tricky melody to sing. The music doesn't just plod along in a monotone fashion, it asks quite a lot of the singer I think. But it's a very stirring hymn.

This is a good hymn that can be sung at both weddings and funerals, two important events in one's life, and this is chosen equally for both wedding ceremonies – as Queen Elizabeth II did for hers – and funerals. It gives you great comfort when you sing it, with words like 'Yea, though I walk in death's dark vale / Yet will I fear no ill / For thou are with me, and thy rod / And staff me comfort still.' It's very direct in its message.

I'm often asked to play hymns on my *Good Morning Sunday* programme on BBC Radio 2 and this hymn is very near the top of the request list. It's usually asked for to remember a passed away loved one or to herald a forthcoming wedding. Interestingly, it's not the *Crimond* tune that people want to hear; what's become obvious through all the emails that do come in to me is that it's actually the tune *Brother James' Air*, *Marosa* that people associate most with their weddings and funerals. The most bizarre recording of 'The Lord's My Shepherd' was sent to me at Radio 2. It was The Rhymney Silvrian Male Choir singing the words of the hymn to the tune of 'Amazing Grace'! I played it, hand on heart, the first time to create a reaction. It did – my listeners loved it and still request it to this day!

'The Lord's My Shepherd' is very metric in its construction and I have to admit that I've heard it murdered in many a parish church, when the organist doesn't really get the whole timing of the music. But it's a hymn that when it's performed well can be fantastically moving. I suppose it's not performed as often these days because I think you've actually got to be quite a good musician to carry it off. Needless to say it sounded pretty dreadful when we sang it in Llandegfan Primary School! But at least it was sung with feeling!

It's funny how certain hymns work their way into your very being. When I was a choirboy at Bangor Cathedral, I remember singing services on a Tuesday evening, a Thursday evening, rehearsals on a Friday, rehearsals on a Saturday, then two services on a Sunday. You'd get to that Sunday evensong service and all of a sudden you'd realize that it was the hymn 'The Lord's My Shepherd' that you were singing and you were on familiar territory. You could give it your all and sing it out joyfully.

Amazing when you think that this hymn has only been included in *The Anglican Hymnbook* since 1965. For me it feels that it's been around since Psalm 23 and that people have been singing it for thousands of generations.

36

O JESUS I HAVE PROMISED

Words: John Ernest Bode (1816–74)
Music: James William Elliott (1833–1915): *Day of Rest*
Arthur H. Mann (1850–1929): *Angel's Story*
Basil Harwood (1859–1949): *Thornbury*
Geoffrey Beaumont (1903–1970): *Hatherop Castle*
William Harold Ferguson (1874–1950): *Wolvercote*

O Jesus, I have promised
To serve thee to the end;
Be thou for ever near me,
My master and my friend:
I shall not fear the battle
If thou art by my side,
Nor wander from the pathway
If thou wilt be my guide.

O let me feel thee near me:
The world is ever near;
I see the sights that dazzle,
The tempting sounds I hear;
My foes are ever near me,
Around me and within;
But, Jesus, draw thou nearer,
And shield my soul from sin.

O let me hear thee speaking
In accents clear and still,
Above the storms of passion,
The murmurs of self-will;
O speak to reassure me,
To hasten or control;
O speak, and make me listen,
Thou guardian of my soul.

O Jesus, thou hast promised
To all who follow thee,
That where thou art in glory
There shall thy servant be;
And, Jesus, I have promised
To serve thee to the end:
O give me grace to follow,
My master and my friend.

O let me see thy foot-marks,
And in them plant mine own;
My hope to follow duly
Is in thy strength alone;
O guide me, call me, draw me,
Uphold me to the end,
And then in heaven receive me,
My Saviour and my friend.

'O JESUS I HAVE PROMISED' was first published as 'A Hymn for the newly confirmed'; and it was written for that purpose. I first got to know this hymn, as has been the case with nearly all of my top forty, as a child and then as a chorister at Bangor Cathedral. I have loved it ever since. I feel that the words draw you closer to Jesus as your friend. There have been many melodies written to complement these fine comforting words, some in my view more successful than others.

John Ernest Bode wrote the words. He was the son of William Bode, 'late of the General Post Office'. William Bode gave his son the best education: he went to Eton, then to the Charter House, followed by Christ Church, Oxford. Ordained in 1841, he was Rector of Westwell, Oxfordshire from 1847 until 1860, when he went to live and work at Castle Camps, Cambridgeshire. It was there that he wrote 'O Jesus I Have Promised' in 1869 for the confirmation of his three children.

Revd Bode was considered a fine scholar. In 1855, he had the privilege of giving the Oxford Bampton Lectures on Divinity. (Reginald Heber, author of 'Holy! Holy! Holy!', was another Bampton lecturer.) He was also a respected poet. His published works included *Ballads from Herodotus* and *Short Occasional Poems*. In 1857, he just missed becoming Poetry Professor at Oxford, being narrowly defeated by Matthew Arnold.

Bode also wrote hymns, including 'God of Heaven, Enthroned in Might' and for Whit Sunday, 'Spirit of Truth, in Dwelling Light'. But 'O Jesus I Have Promised' is his only truly lasting work, and it has kept its popularity – it was 22nd in the BBC *Songs of Praise* poll in 2002. He based his hymn on John 12:26: 'If any man serve me, let him follow me; and where I am, there shall also my servant be . . .' It was printed first as an SPCK (Society for the Propogation of Christian Knowledge) leaflet, and later in *Hymns Ancient and Modern*, 1875 edition, set to *Day of Rest* by J. W. Elliott. This isn't a tune I ever associated with Bode's words, and it's only through researching this book that I got to know and appreciate this lovely tune.

James William Elliott is celebrated for his popular scores for his *Nursery Rhymes and Nursery Songs*, but he was also an all-round expert in church music. His musical education began as a child chorister. He was organist and choirmaster, composer of hymns and service music – and he was Sir Arthur Sullivan's assistant in the editing of Sullivan's *Church Hymns with Tunes*. He wrote the setting for 'O Jesus I Have Promised' originally for Christopher Wordsworth's hymn 'O day of rest and gladness'.

As a chorister I also never sang the tune by Arthur H. Mann although I know that it is very popular. Mann's background is steeped in choral sacred music. He was a chorister and assistant organist at Norwich Cathedral. He was organist at King's College Chapel, Cambridge from 1876 to 1929. As well as composing an oratorio and a number of hymn tunes, he was also musical editor of *The Church of England Hymnal*. His musical setting for this hymn is called *Angel's Story*, a lovely hymn title if ever there was one.

Basil Harwood, who was born the youngest of twelve children in Gloucestershire in 1859, composed one of my favourite tunes, used for this hymn. He was educated at Trinity College, Oxford and went on to St Barnabas Church in Pimlico in London, Ely Cathedral and Christ Church, Oxford. He co-founded and conducted the Oxford Bach Choir. He also was a precentor of Keble College, Oxford and was music editor of the 1909 *Oxford Hymn Book*. He loved to walk and would name many of his hymn tunes after local places he enjoyed visiting. His remains are interred in St Barnabas Church, Pimlico and marked by a plaque inset in the floor of the chancel, close to where he would have stood to conduct the choir. He wrote many fine hymn tunes including 'Let All The World In Every Corner Sing'. His melody

Thornbury is also sung to the words 'Thy Hand O God has Guided', but I think that this melody serves 'O Jesus I Have Promised' just as well. It's a lovely tune.

Anglican priest and composer Geoffrey Beaumont wrote a modern version I also enjoy. He was chaplain of Trinity College, Cambridge. Beaumont co-founded the 20th Century Church Light Music Group and edited several collections of new hymns and songs, many of which found their way into hymnbooks around the world and are still sung today. If you're feeling down in the dumps this melody really does uplift you. His tune is called *Hatherop Castle* and even though I don't sing this tune often I particularly enjoy hearing it performed by the International Staff Band of the Salvation Army.

And finally we come to my favourite tune for the hymn. It is the setting of the Revd William Harold Ferguson's *Wolvercote*, printed in *The Public School Hymnbook* of 1919, when Ferguson was chaplain and musical director of Lancing College. Its public school, Establishment associations have maybe limited its popularity of late, but it's a very fine tune. Even though I went to David Hughes Comprehensive School on Anglesey (most definitely not a public school) this hymn tune is one I used to sing often. I think this gorgeous melody suits the words just brilliantly. The tune is such a joy to sing as it moves about quite a bit and the change of 'feel' on the line 'I shall not fear the battle' is just sublime. There are certain hymn tunes that make you feel great when you sing them and for me this is one of them. This hymn of dedication and commitment is a cracker.

37

ALL GLORY LAUD AND HONOUR

Words: St Theodulph of Orleans (*c.*750–821)
English version: J. M. Neale (1818–66)
Music: Melchior Teschner (1584–1635)

All glory, laud, and honour
To thee, Redeemer, King,
To whom the lips of children
Made sweet hosannas ring.

Thou are the King of Israel,
Thou David's royal Son,
Who in the Lord's name comest,
The King and Blessed One.

The company of angels
Are praising thee on high,
And mortal men and all things
Created make reply.

The people of the Hebrews
With palms before thee went;
Our praise and prayer and anthems
Before thee we present.

To thee, before thy Passion,
They sang their hymns of praise;
To thee, now high exalted,
Our melody we raise.

Thou didst accept their praises;
Accept the prayers we bring,
Who in all good delightest,
Thou good and gracious King.

All glory, laud, and honour
To thee, Redeemer, King,
To whom the lips of children
Made sweet hosannas ring.

WITH SOME the greatest hymns that we now sing worldwide, words and music were not written at the same time, or by the same person. This stately Palm Sunday processional hymn is a splendid example of this. Its words were written down right at the beginning of the seventh century and its music centuries later in 1615 – it's one of the oldest melodies we've got here in the top forty. So powerful are its words that they are said to have secured the release of their author from gaol.

St Theodulph was born in Italy. He was brought to France by Charlemagne and was consecrated Bishop of Orleans in about 785. Theodulph was a welcome member of the court around Charlemagne, but was not so popular with Charlemagne's successor the Emperor Louis (Louis the Pious), who had Theodulph imprisoned for conspiracy against him in 1818.

In prison at Angers, Theodulph wrote this Palm Sunday processional hymn, which celebrates Christ's entry into Jerusalem on a donkey (from Matthew 21.1–17, in the Latin original: 'Gloria, laus et honor tibi sit, rex Christe redemptor'). On Palm Sunday in 821, Louis the Pious passed in procession below Theodulph's cell window. Theodulph took this opportunity to sing his hymn to the Emperor, who was so moved by it that he had Theodulph released. True or not, this story has no happy ending, for Theodulph died later that year.

The version of the hymn sung today is in the fine translation by John Mason Neale for his 1852 book *Mediaeval Hymns*. J. M. Neale was a Tractarian and supporter of the Oxford Movement, whose members in the mid-nineteenth century set out to restore to the Church of England its medieval, Catholic inheritance. He was a prolific translator of hymns and carols (including 'Good King Wenceslas'), often finding his sources in Latin hymnals and the Greek Orthodox Church. He was also a busy worker in the Church – he founded an order of nuns and oversaw a refuge for indigent old men.

Neale selected the verses we sing today from Theodulph's multi-verse original. He also mentioned the deletion in the seventeenth century for, as he put it, its 'quaintness', of this verse:

> Be thou, O Lord, the rider,
> And we the little ass,
> That to God's holy city,
> Together we may pass.

The hymn is sung to the tune of *St Theodulph*, written by Melchior Teschner (1584–1635). The German composer studied theology, philosophy and music at Frankfurt an der

Oder. He became cantor at Smigiel and after further study was cantor and pastor at Fraustadt in Germany. J. S. Bach liked the melody, and incorporated it into the *St John Passion*.

'All Glory Laud and Honour' has found its place in Palm Sunday processions, with the opening verses sung by a group of boy choristers, to be repeated by the whole congregation. We sang it in the Bangor Cathedral choir and it has remained with me into adulthood. Even though it's a Palm Sunday hymn, it makes me think of Christmas, because it reminds me of a Welsh nursery rhyme called 'pwy sy'n dwad dros y bryn yn ddistaw ddistaw bach?', that I used to sing with my parents as a small child while we were waiting for the arrival of the great man himself, Father Christmas.

It roughly translates as 'who's coming over the hill really quietly? He's got a long beard and white hair, and he's got something in his sack'. The melody of this nursery rhyme is reminiscent of 'All Glory Laud and Honour' and we used to have quite a few giggles in Bangor Cathedral choir when we sang this at Easter because we thought it really should be sung at Christmas. Forgive me, I was very young!

Each verse beautifully describes a chapter in Jesus' life. My favourite verse to sing is:

> To thee, before thy Passion,
> They sang their hymns of praise;
> To thee, now high exalted,
> Our melody we raise.

There is also something quite magical about the words

> To whom the lips of children
> Made sweet hosannas ring

I love the fact that these hosannas were sweet anyway – but He made them ring!

This hymn is all about praising and praying. And as with many hymns in this list it is very repetitive. It acknowledges Christ as the King, from child King to a good and gracious King, and reinforces the fact that we should praise his word and try to live good lives. In short we should obey the King.

38

GREAT IS THY FAITHFULNESS

Words: Thomas O. Chisholm (1866–1960)
Music: William Runyan (1870–1957)

Great is thy faithfulness, O God my Father,
There is no shadow of turning with thee;
Thou changest not, thy compassions they fail not,
As thou has been thou for ever will be.

Great is thy faithfulness!
Great is thy faithfulness!
Morning by morning new mercies I see;
All I have needed thy hand hath provided;
Great is thy faithfulness, Lord, unto me!

Summer and winter, and springtime and harvest,
Sun, moon and stars in their courses above
Join with all nature in manifold witness
To thy great faithfulness, mercy and love.

Chorus

Pardon for sin and a peace that endureth
Thine own dear presence to cheer and to guide;
Strength for today and bright hope for tomorrow,
Blessings all mine, with ten thousand beside!

Chorus

'GREAT IS THY FAITHFULNESS' is the quintessential twentieth-century hymn. Its words and music were written in the 1920s, it reached a wide audience through the new media of radio and television and was brought to millions by the crusade ministry of a great twentieth-century Evangelist.

The hymn's author and composer were friends. Methodist minister Thomas Obadiah Chisholm wrote the verses of 'Great is Thy Faithfulness' in 1923. He was born in a log cabin in Simpson County, Kentucky, and came to the ministry from jobs in school teaching and journalism. Just a year into his ministry, his health failing, he had to give up his pastoral duties and went on to earn his living in the life insurance business.

Thomas Chisholm made a generous contribution to church music: he wrote a great number of poems and many of them became hymns. 'Great is Thy Faithfulness' is the most famous of these. Alongside his love of the Bible and its teaching, he put his own daily life into its verses. His source for verse one is Lamentations 3:22 and 3:33, which declares resoundingly: 'His compassions fail not. They are new every morning: great is thy faithfulness'.

His friend William Runyan was the son of a Methodist minister and himself a devout Methodist. He was in those days well known as a composer of gospel songs and sacred music. Chisholm sent him the poem and Runyan set it to the tune 'Faithfulness'.

Runyan had connections to the Moody Bible Institute, which was founded in 1866 by the evangelist, educationist – and businessman – Dwight Lyman Moody. Its declared purpose was 'the education and training of Christian workers, including teachers, ministers, missionaries and musicians who may completely and effectively proclaim the gospel of Jesus Christ'. The campus Moody set down in downtown Chicago is there still. This was the first American religious institution to spread its teaching through the power of radio: WMBI, 'the power house of Evangelical radio' and the first non-commercial radio station in America, went on air in 1926. Today it's a major Network. 'Great is Thy Faithfulness' was broadcast on WMBI's morning programme 'Hymns from the Chapel', and one of the singers on that show was George Beverly Shea (1909–).

Together Billy Graham and 'America's Beloved Gospel Singer' George Beverly Shea took an Evangelical Christianity and its music and made them mainstream. The fine Canadian bass-baritone gospel singer became a featured soloist for Billy Graham on Graham's WCFL radio program 'Songs in the Night'. Through his radio career, a huge audience – estimated at over 220 million – tuned in to hear him live. 'Great is Thy Faithfulness' was one of his most popular and loved hymns, alongside 'How Great Thou Art'. From 1947, he took the hymn out into Billy Graham's famed Evangelical crusades and Shea sang it during the crusade that came to Haringay, north London in 1954.

Today 'Great is Thy Faithfulness' ranks high in the *Songs of Praise* polls. I honestly believe this is the case because it's so easy to sing. Even though the melody dances around quite a bit, performing this majestic hymn really does make you feel good – especially, as is often the case on *Songs of Praise*, when being accompanied by organ, woodwind and brass band.

39

ONWARD CHRISTIAN SOLDIERS

Words: Sabine Baring-Gould (1834–1924)
Music: Arthur Sullivan (1842–1900)

Onward, Christian soldiers,
Marching as to war,
With the Cross of Jesus
Going on before.
Christ the Royal Master
Leads against the foe;
Forward into battle,
See his banners go!

Onward, Christian soldiers,
Marching as to war,
With the Cross of Jesus
Going on before.

At the sin of triumph
Satan's host doth flee:
On then, Christian soldiers,
On to victory.
Hell's foundations quiver
At the shout of praise;
Brothers, lift your voices,
Loud your anthems raise.

Chorus

Like a mighty army,
Moves the church of God;
Brothers, we are treading
Where the saints have trod;
We are not divided
All one body we,
One in hope and doctrine,
One in charity.

Chorus

Crowns and thrones may perish,
Kingdoms rise and wane,
But the church of Jesus
Constant will remain;
Gates of hell can never
'Gainst that church prevail;
We have Christ's own promise,
And that cannot fail.

Chorus

Onward, then, ye people,
Join our happy throng,
Blend with ours your voices
In the triumph song;
Glory, laud and honour
Unto Christ the king,
This through countless ages
Men and angels sing.

> Onward, Christian soldiers,
> Marching as to war,
> With the Cross of Jesus
> Going on before.

YOU CAN GAUGE the popularity of a hymn if it's been used in the cartoon series *The Simpsons*. This hymn has (as has another of my top forty), and in my book it's a good hymn. However, I am owning up that I haven't yet recorded it. Nor have I sung it in a live setting, either in a church or a cathedral or as part of a *Songs of Praise* congregation. Yet I think that it's probably one of the most rousing hymns going and a great call to join the fellowship to worship God. These days it's associated with war, and armies, and marching but we should take into account that it wasn't written in the mid-nineteenth century to be used in that context, but for children processing to church in the parish of Horbury Bridge in Yorkshire.

It's struck me in researching the hymns in this book, that all the best, most recognizable of them seem to have been written in the space of ten minutes or less. This is one such hymn. Its author Sabine Baring-Gould confessed that, 'It was written in great haste, and I am afraid some of the rhymes are faulty.' The words and the music are not in the least faulty and they really do fit in with the style of the piece. Add to them a brass band or an orchestral accompaniment, and what you have here is probably the ultimate stirring hymn.

Sabine Baring-Gould was born in Exeter in 1834. His education was not strictly conventional because his family travelled through Europe during his childhood, but he still managed to gain two degrees at Cambridge before he became the curate at Horbury Bridge. His marriage was also rather unconventional – and a success story; in Horbury Bridge he met and fell in love with Grace Taylor, the sixteen-year-old daughter of a mill hand. Grace was obviously not quite up to scratch for a curate's wife, so Baring-Gould sent her to live for two years with a vicar's family in York to learn proper manners, then married her in 1868, to the shock and disapproval of both families. However their marriage lasted for forty-eight years, and the couple had fifteen children. When he buried his wife in 1916, Baring-Gould had carved on her tombstone the beautiful Latin motto *Dimidium Animae Meae* ('Half My Soul').

He was by all accounts a very fine preacher and the fact that his sermons lasted only ten minutes indicated he was obviously a man ahead of his time. I think we would have got on. He was surprised that his hymn became so popular, and it has, despite all the controversy over its content and meaning. It is the Salvation Army's favoured processional hymn and it came 26th in the 2005 *Songs of Praise* poll. But 'Onward Christian Soldiers' has also been dropped from several modern hymnbooks due to the supposed militaristic leanings I've described. There have also been several attempts to rewrite it for a more contemporary audience, including Christian lesbians and gay men's 'Onward, Christian Homos, Marching Out With Pride' (written by Derek Rawcliffe, former Bishop of Glasgow) and a pacifist version drafted by David Wright in the aftermath of the Falklands War begins: 'Onward, Christian pilgrims, / Working hard for peace / Day by day we're praying / That all wars may cease.' Despite the new words of these versions, they seem to share with the original the themes of being united to a cause and moving forward together.

Rather than glorifying war, the words of the hymn can be seen as a stirring call for Christians to unite and follow Christ. According to this view, the words are metaphorical – 'like a mighty army', 'marching as to war' – and the hymn expresses the idea of the Church militant, exhorting believers not to fight but to move forward in faith and to directly engage with the world's threats rather than retreat from them, with 'At the sign of triumph, Satan's host doth flee'. Its direct words and marching tune have had a strong effect in stirring and uniting those who are singing it and this is perhaps one reason why it has remained so popular – in whichever version it is sung.

But with such rousing words and so clear a tune, it's not surprising that there have been many parodies of the hymn. One of these expresses the frustration of Church reformers: 'Like a mighty tortoise,' this goes, 'Moves the Church of God; Brothers, we are treading, Where we've always trod!'

I have always been open in my dislike for the operettas of Gilbert and Sullivan. But here I can acknowledge that Sullivan has created a hymn for the masses to enjoy. A real *tour de force*.

Sabine Baring-Gould wrote it originally to a tune adapted from Haydn's Symphony No.53 but the melody we now use was written by Arthur Sullivan in 1871. Like Gould, who wrote the words at speed, apparently Sullivan dashed off the tune in a hurry. He was staying at the country house in Dorset of Gertrude Clay-Ker-Symer and he named it *St Gertrude* after his hostess. It was published in *The Hymnary*, Novello, 1872 and was an instant success. She must have been a very fine hostess!

'Onward Christian Soldiers' has also been a huge favourite

with filmmakers and TV producers. The tendency in putting it on screen has been to support either one or the other of the two opposing views of the hymn itself. In the wartime movie *Mrs Miniver* (1942), for example, it's sung by the congregation at the film's end as an inspiration to fight in World War II, with planes forming V for Victory visible through the roof of the bombed church. In the film of *M*A*S*H* (1970), on the other hand, it becomes a caustic comment on the futility of war.

Winston Churchill and Franklin Roosevelt met in 1941 on the battleship HMS *Prince of Wales* to agree the Atlantic Charter. A church service was held and Prime Minister Churchill chose the hymns. He chose 'Onward Christian Soldiers'. He later went onto the radio to explain why he chose it. 'We sang "Onward Christian Soldiers" indeed, and I felt that this was no vain presumption, but that we had the right to feel that we serving a cause for the sake of which a trumpet has sounded from on high. When I looked upon that densely packed congregation of fighting men of the same language, of the same faith, of the same fundamental laws, of the same ideals . . . it swept across me that here was the only hope, but also the sure hope, of saving the world from measureless degradation.'

BATTLE HYMN OF THE REPUBLIC – GLORY, GLORY, HALLELUJAH

Words: Julia Ward Howe (1819–1910)
Music: William Steffe (1830–1890)

Mine eyes have seen the glory of the coming of the
    Lord:
He is trampling out the vintage where the grapes of
    wrath are stored;
He hath loosed the fateful lightning of His terrible
    swift sword:
His truth is marching on.

Glory, glory, hallelujah!
Glory, glory, hallelujah!
Glory, glory, hallelujah!
His truth is marching on.

I have seen Him in the watch-fires of a hundred
    circling camps,
They have builded Him an altar in the evening dews
    and damps;
I can read His righteous sentence by the dim and
    flaring lamps:
His day is marching on.

Chorus

I have read a fiery gospel writ in burnished rows of
    steel:
'As ye deal with my condemners, so with you my grace
    shall deal;
Let the Hero, born of woman, crush the serpent with
    his heel,
Since God is marching on.'

Chorus

He has sounded forth the trumpet that shall never call
    retreat;
He is sifting out the hearts of men before His
    judgment-seat:
Oh, be swift, my soul, to answer Him! be jubilant, my
    feet!
Our God is marching on.

Chorus

In the beauty of the lilies Christ was born across the
    sea,
With a glory in His bosom that transfigures you and
    me:
As He died to make men holy, let us die to make men
    free,
While God is marching on.

Chorus

He is coming like the glory of the morning on the
   wave,
He is wisdom to the mighty, He is succour to the
   brave,
So the world shall be His footstool, and the soul of
   Time His slave,
Our God is marching on.

Chorus

THIS NOW ANTHEMIC piece of music, written in the
mid-nineteenth century by William Steffe, started as a
humble campfire song: 'Say brothers, will you meet us / On
Caanan's happy shore'. So it remained, and carried on
accumulating quite a few more sets of lyrics, until early in the
American Civil War it was adopted for the Union marching
song 'John Brown's Body' and this version stuck. Then in
1862, Julia Ward Howe of South Boston set out to write new
words to the tune. She tells us what happened: she had gone
to bed and had slept soundly, then, 'I awoke in the grey of the
morning twilight; and as I lay waiting for the dawn, the long
lines of the desired poem began to twine themselves in my
mind. Having thought out all the stanzas, I said to myself, I
must get up and write these verses down, lest I fall asleep
again and forget them. So, with a sudden effort, I sprang out
of bed, and found in the dimness an old stump of a pen which
I remembered to have used the day before. I scrawled the
verses almost without looking at the paper.'* Her version, set

---

*Julia Ward Howe, *Reminiscences: 1819-1899*, Houghton Mifflin, New York,
1899

to Steffe's music, was first published in the *New York Daily Tribune* in January 1882, swiftly followed by the *Atlantic Monthly* under its new title 'The Battle Hymn of the Republic'.

Julia Ward Howe was a Unitarian and she shared the Northern States' antipathy to the slave system of the South. She has written a true 'battle hymn' favouring the Union soldiers in that war: with Christ present among the 'watch-fires of a hundred circling camps' and 'evening dews and damps' and with the challenge, 'As He died to make men holy, let us die to make men free'. Perhaps such a sentiment was too militant for *Songs of Praise*, which published the hymn with the heading, 'For Secular use', and many hymnals today have tweaked this line to: 'As He died to make men holy, let us *live* to make *us* free'.

And it's not an easy one to sing. I performed this hymn with Katherine Jenkins and Bryn Terfel as part of Bryn Terfel's Faenol Festival in North Wales. We were recording a *Songs of Praise* special there and Katherine, Bryn and myself were sharing the performance of 'Battle Hymn of the Republic', taking a verse each. To think that between us we'd probably sung on every major platform in the world, here were three Welsh people really struggling with a performance of this hymn that started life in America. Katherine and myself actually started to giggle! All very unprofessional! It seems to me that there are too many words for the verses and this affects the rhythm, so that you have to spit them out. It can all begin to sound very mechanical. If you don't breathe proper-ly throughout then you're constantly playing catch-up. But then, with some relief, you get to the chorus and sing 'Glory Glory Hallelujah, Glory Glory Hallelujah, Glory Glory

Hallelujah, His truth is marching on'. It's such a blessed relief! It's the chorus that energises this patriotic hymn, there's nothing else like it.

Elvis has performed the hymn to great effect and the Mormon Tabernacle Choir made it their own in the 1960s. It's also been in the charts, reaching No 13 in the Billboard Top 100. I have to say that this hymn almost didn't make it into my top forty because of its associations with Manchester United football team. As an Arsenal supporter, it's quite difficult for me to hear the 'Glory Glory Man United' part of the hymn! But it's scraped into the top forty because of its place in history and also the fact that the great chorus is enjoyed by so many people worldwide.

In view of its history, it's not maybe surprising that the lyrics of 'Battle Hymn of the Republic' were used by Martin Luther King in his speeches, as well as in his final sermon 'I've been to the Mountaintop', given in Memphis on 3 April, 1968, the night before his assassination.

REFERENCES

BOOKS

Jonathan Aitken, *John Newton: From Disgrace to Amazing Grace* (Crossway Books, 2007)

John Betjeman, *Sweet Songs of Zion* (Hodder & Stoughton, 2008)

Ian Bradley, *The Daily Telegraph Book of Hymns* (Continuum, 2005)

Henry Chadwick (ed.), *Not Angels, But Anglicans: A History of Christianity in the British Isles* (Canterbury Press, 2000)

J. Irving Erickson, *Sing It Again* (Covenant Publications, 1985)

J. Irving Erickson, *Twice Born Hymns* (Covenant Publications, 1976)

J. T. Fowler, *Life and Letters of John Bacchus Dykes* (1897, reprinted 2001)

Henry James Garland, *Henry Francis Lyte and the story of 'Abide with Me'* (Torch Publishing, 1957)

John Julian, *Dictionary of Hymnology: Origin and History of Christian Hymns and Hymnwriters of all ages and nations* (John Murray, 1915)

Graham Kendrick, Gerald Coates, Roger Forster and Lynne Green with Catherine Butcher, *March for Jesus* (Kingsway, 1992)

Marjorie Reeves and Jenyth Worsley, *Favourite Hymns: 200 Years of Magnificat* (2001)

Vincent B. Sherry, *The Cambridge Companion to the Literature of the First World War* (Cambridge University Press, 2005)

Steve Turner, *'Amazing Grace': The Story of America's Most Beloved Song* (Ecco/HarperCollins, 2002)

J. R. Watson (ed.), *An Annotated Anthology of Hymns* (Oxford University Press, 2003)

A Historical Dictionary of British Women (Routledge, 2003)

The Catholic Encyclopedia (1909)

ACKNOWLEDGEMENTS

Firstly, to my family for their support, love and unquestioning faith . . . especially to Emilia and Lucas who occasionally had to cut short a spirited game as it was distracting! Love and thanks to Philippa Brewster for her unstinting enthusiasm, encouragement and helping hand. To Hugh Faupel, my mate, for his thought and care. To Georgina Capel and Anita Land for being the wicked sisters! To Wendi Batt for being an angel – thanks. To Trevor Dolby, Nicola Taplin and all at Preface and Random House – thanks for having me on board, it makes me very proud. To Peter Ward for the text design and Two Associates for the jacket. To all at *Songs of Praise*, thanks for the great times. To Brian Berg and all at Universal TV who will be releasing my hymn album. And a huge thanks to all the authors and composers who have given us these musical gems. Keep singing!